Foreign Trade and Foreign Exchange

P. Komaladevi,

Assistant Professor,

Department of Commerce,

Gobi Arts & Science College,

Gobichettipalayam.

Published by

Foreign Trade and Foreign Exchange

ISBN 978-93-87862-05-0

Author

P. Komaladevi

Bonfring

309, 2nd Floor,

5th Street Extension, Gandhipuram,

Coimbatore-641 012.

Tamilnadu, India.

E-mail: info@bonfring.org

Website: www.bonfring.org

Phone: 0422 4213231

FOREIGN TRADE

Meaning

Trade between two or more nations is called foreign trade or international trade. Foreign trade is also known as external trade. This involves the exchange of goods and services between the citizens of two nations. When the citizens of one nation exchange goods and services with the citizens of another nation, it is called foreign trade

Scope of Foreign Trade

i) Uneven Distribution of Natural Resources

Natural resources of the world are not evenly divided amongst the nations of the world. Different countries of the world have different amount of natural resources and they differ with each other in regard to climate, minerals and other factors. So they have to depend upon one another for the exchange of their surpluses with the goods is in short in their country and hence the need for foreign trade is natural.

ii) Division of Labour and Specialization

Due to uneven distribution of natural resources, some countries are more suitable placed to produce some goods more economically than other countries. But they are geographically at a disadvantageous position to produce other goods. They specialize in the production of such goods in which they have some natural advantage in the form of availability of raw material, labour, technical know-how, climatic conditions, etc., and get other goods in exchange for these goods from other countries.

iii) Differences in Economic Growth Rate

Some countries are developed, some are developing, while there are some other countries which are under-developed; these under- developed and developing countries have to depend upon developed ones for financial help, which ultimately encourages foreign trade.

iv). Theory of Comparative Cost

According to the theory of comparative cost each country should concentrate on the production of those goods for which it is best suited, taking into account its natural resources, climate, labour supply, technical know-how and the level of development. Each country specializes in the production of those goods which it can produce at the lowest cost as compared to other countries which leads to international specialization and division of labour. This reduces the cost of production all over the world and improves the standard of living of the people in various countries. Hence the theory of comparative cost encourages foreign trade.

Need for Foreign Trade

There are several reasons for going foreign trade. There is an increasing demand for foreign trade because of the following reasons:

1. Profit Motive

One of the most important objectives of foreign trade is the profit advantage. International business could be more profitable than the domestic. One of the important motivations for foreign investment is to reduce the cost of production. Even where, international business is less profitable than the domestic. It could increase the total profit. In certain cases, international business can help increase the profitability of the domestic business.

2. Growth Opportunities

The enormous growth potential of many foreign markets is a very strong attraction for foreign companies. In a number of developing countries, both the population and income are growing fast. It may be noted that several developing countries have been growing much faster than the developed countries. Even if the market for several goods is not substantial, many companies are eager to establish a foot holds there, considering their future potential.

3. Domestic Market Constraints

Domestic demand countries drive many companies to expanding the market beyond the national borders. The market for a number of products declines in the advanced countries. This happens when the market potential has been almost fully tapped. Another type of domestic market constraint arises from the scale of operation substantially in many industries marking it necessary to have foreign market, in addition to the domestic market, to take advantage of the scale economies.

4. Competition

Competition may become a driving force behind international trade. A protected market does not normally motivate companies to seek business outside the home market. Many companies take an offering international competitive strategy by way of countries-competition. The economic liberalisation has increased competition from foreign firms as well as from those within the country has changed the scene.

5. Government Policies and Regulation

Government policies and regulations may also motivate foreign trade. There are bolt positive and negative factors which could cause foreign trade. Many countries give a number of incentives and other positive support to domestic companies to export and to invest in foreign countries. Similarly several countries give a lot of importance to import development and foreign investment. Many Indian companies are entering international market because of positive reasons.

6. Monopoly Power

Monopoly power may a size from such factors as monopolisation of certain resources, patent rights, technological advantage, product differentiation etc., such monopoly power need not necessarily be an absolute one but even a dominant position may facilities internationalisation.

7. Spin-off Benefits

Foreign trade has restrain spin-off benefits too. International business helps improve the image of the company. International marketing may have pay-off for the internal market too be giving the domestic market better products. Further, the foreign exchange earnings may enable a company to import capital goods, technology etc., which may not otherwise be possible in countries like India.

8. Strategic Vision

The systematic and growing internationalisation of many companies is essentially a part of their business policy or strategic management. The stimulus for foreign trade comes from the urge to grow, the need to become more competitive, the need to diversity and to gain strategic advantage of internationalisation. There are a number of corporations which are truly global. Planning of manufacturing facilities logistical systems, financial flows and marketing policies in such corporations is done considering the entire world as its market.

9. Uneven Distribution of Natural Resources

Different countries are differently endowed with natural resources. Climatic conditions also differ among countries. The uneven distribution of the resources and prevalence of varied climatic conditions mean that each country cannot produce all the goods and services it requires.

10. Theory of Comparative Cost

The comparative cost advantage of a country in the production of commodity is measured by the relative value of one commodity in terms of the other. A country has comparative cost advantage in the production of a commodity when it has maximum cost advantages or least cost disadvantage.

Importance of Foreign Trade

In the early stage of human civilization, men produced as per their need and consumption. But the industrial development has made production round about and this has resulted in large scale production. This is turn necessitates and foreign trade which helps in the distribution of surplus produced. The primary objective of foreign trade is to increase production and raise the standard of living of its people.

There is a growing need for foreign trade because of the following reasons

1. It leads to effective and better utilization of natural resources.
2. The uneven distribution of natural resources has resulted foreign trade.
3. It develops a wide range of market for the products.
4. It is regarded as a boon to meet natural calamities like flood, drought.
5. It contributes a great deal of well being of the people involved in foreign trade.

Risks in Foreign Trade

Companies doing business across international borders face many of the same risks as would normally be evident in strictly domestic transactions.

For example,

1. Buyer insolvency
2. Non-acceptance (buyer rejects goods as different from the agreed upon specifications)
3. Credit risk (allowing the buyer to take possession of goods prior to payment)
4. Regulatory risk (e.g., a change in rules that prevents the transaction);
5. Intervention (governmental action to prevent a transaction being completed)
6. Political risk (change in leadership interfering with transactions or prices)
7. War and other uncontrollable events. In addition, foreign trade also faces the risk of unfavorable exchange rate movements.

Advantages of Foreign Trade

1. Increased Standard of Living

It ensures more production to meet the demand of the people of different countries. By increased production, it becomes possible to increase income and the standard of living of its people. It also increases the standard of living by increasing more employment opportunities.

2. Large Scale Production

It ensures large production because the production is carried on to meet the demand of its people as well as world market. Large scale production also ensures a great deal of internal economies which reduces the cost of production.

3. Greater Variety of Goods Available for Consumption

The international trade brings in different varieties of a particular product from different destinations. This gives consumers a wider array of choices which will not only improve their quality of life but as a whole it will help the country grow.

4. Efficient Allocation and Better Utilization of Resources

The efficient allocation and better utilisation of resources of countries tend to produce goods in which they have a comparative advantage. When countries produce through comparative advantage, wasteful duplication of resources is prevented. It helps save the environment from harmful gases being leaked into the atmosphere and also provides countries with a better marketing power.

5. Promotes Efficiency in Production

All the countries will try to adopt better methods of production to keep costs down in order to remain competitive. Countries that can produce a product at the lowest possible cost will be able to gain a larger share in the market. Therefore an incentive to produce efficiently arises. This will help standards of the product to increase and consumers will have a good quality product to consume.

6. More Employment

More employment could be generated as the market for the countries' goods widens through trade. International trade helps generate more employment through the establishment of newer industries to cater to the demands of various countries. This will help countries bring down their unemployment rates.

7. Optimum Use of Resources

Foreign trade helps in the optimum use of natural resources and avoids wastages of resources.

8. Stable Price

It ensures the presence of stable price by avoiding wide fluctuations in prices. It tries to equalise the world price.

9. Availability of All Types of Goods

It enables a country to import those goods which it cannot produce.

Disadvantages of Foreign Trade

Foreign trade is not free from difficulties. The following are some of the important difficulties of foreign trade:

1. Problem of Distance

It is a long distance trade and as such it becomes difficult to maintain close relationship between the buyer and the seller.

2. Language Problem

An international market encounters problems arising out of the differences in the language. Even when the same language is used in different countries, the same words or terms may have different meanings or connotations. The language problem, however, is not something peculiar to the international marketing. The multiplicity of languages in India is an example.

3. Procedural Difficulties

Foreign trade involves preparation of a number of documents which also creates difficulties in the way of foreign trade.

4. Restrictions on Trade

Some restrictions are imposed on export and import of commodities. These restrictions stand on the progress of foreign trade.

5. Greater Risks

Foreign trade involves a great deal of risks because trade takes place over a long distance. Though the risks are covered through insurance, it involves extra cost of production because insurance cost is added to cost.

6. Rapid Depletion of Natural Resources

It could lead to a more rapid depletion of exhaustible natural resources. As countries begin to up their production levels, natural resources tend to get.

7. The Political and Legal Differences

The political and legal environment of foreign markets is different from that of the domestic. The complexity generally increases as the number of countries in which a company does business. It should also be noted that the political and legal environment is not the same in all provinces of many home markets.

8. Cultural Differences

The Cultural difference is one of the most difficult problems in international marketing. The cultural environment encompassing the religious aspects, language, customs, traditions and beliefs, tastes and preferences, social stratification, social intuition buying and consumption habits are the very import factors for business. The social and cultural environments of different markets differ vastly. Even within a nation, cultural diversity may be very significant.

9. Economic Differences

The nature and level of development of the economy, economy resources, size of the economy, economic system and policies, economic conditions, trends in the GNP growth rate and per capita income, nature of and trends in foreign trade, domestic supply and demand conditions are all factors relevant to business. All these show that the economic environment of different countries is not similar indicating that different business strategies may be required for the different markets.

10. Differences in Currency Unit

The currency unit varies from nation to nation. This may sometimes cause problems of currency convertibility, besides the problems of exchange rate fluctuations. The monetary system and regulations may also vary.

11. Differences in the Marketing Infrastructure

The availability and nature of the marketing facilities available in different countries may vary widely. For example, an advertising medium very effective in one market may not be available or may be under developed in another market.

Importance of Foreign Trade in Economic Development

Foreign trade has a vital role to play in the economic development of a nation. It has assumed enormous importance and significance in modern days because of the growing specialization and territorial division of labor and consequent inter-dependence of economics.

A developing economy has to break the vicious circle of poverty, attain self-sustained growth and transform itself into an industrialized one from the agrarian level. For this, it requires resources which can be had only through foreign trade, viz., through imports and exports. According to Herberler, foreign trade enables economic development by making available the following factors:

1. Capital through international investment;
2. Means of development in the form or raw materials, goods and machinery;
3. Technology know-how

Apart from these important factors for economic development, exports constitute the key factor in deciding the sustained rate of economic growth Countries have to create export surplus by specializing factor endowments and producing on a large scale with minimum cost.

Further, export industries, in their turn, stimulate home industries and increase their productivity. Export trade plays a dynamic role in converting the domestic resources into more productive forms of capital and machinery and thereby helps capital formation quickly. The process of capital formation will be direct and immediate if the import bills are paid from current export earnings. Export sector serves as a propulsive sector in the process of economic development.

From the point of view of domestic buyer, export surplus is of considerable significance. The domestic consumer will have the freedom of choice to buy in the best competitive market; whereas, when imports are financed by foreign aid, the prices will be marked up by the sellers as they know the buyer has no choice.

Differences between Domestic and International Trade

Trade means exchange of goods and services for the satisfaction of human wants. The process of exchange includes purchase of goods and services and their sale. The trade may take place within geographical boundaries of countries or may be extended to across the border. When trade is confined to the geographical limits of a country, it is a domestic or national trade. In national trade both the buyer and the seller are of the same countries and they enter into trade-agreements subject to the national laws, practices and customs of trade. But foreign trade refers to the trade between two countries. Purchaser and seller are citizens of two different countries and are subject to International or bilateral laws of trade and tariffs. Technically, domestic trade and international trade are more or less identical and are based on the same basic principles of trades. There are certain similarities between domestic and international business in terms of broad objectives and goals of the company, namely: – Generating revenue. – Corporate image and brand building. – Customer satisfaction and building loyalty as patronage buyers. –Carrying out their operations by respecting and adhering to local regulations. – Generation of employment opportunities. But practically, there are certain differences between domestic and foreign trade. The main differences are as follows:

1. Environment

The economic, political, legal, socio-cultural, competitive and technology environments are well known in case of domestic business due to the familiarity of geography and place of operations, hence the organization can take the necessary precautions to assess its impact and adjust quickly to the changes in the same. In international operations the various aspects of the macro external environment are not fully known unless the business is established and created a place for itself in the market. Thus a number of innumerable hidden environmental factors may emerge during the settlement period which may pose problems.

2. Plan and Strategy

Plans and strategies are generally worked out for the short term. The short term plans are linked together and carried forward into the long run. The inverse is also possible as domestic business offers the flexibility to organizations. In case of international business only a well thought out, proven, practical long term time-bound planning and strategy works.

3. Competition

The competitive forces operating in the domestic business environment are restricted to a local boundary. The movement of competitive forces can thus be analyzed and understood more clearly. In case of international business competitive forces are not restricted to a local boundary. They extend over several countries, thereby making it difficult to analyze their motive and movement.

4. Difference in Currencies

There is only one currency acceptable all over the country and therefore there are no difficulties in making payments in internal trade. But, each country has its own monetary system which differs from others. Exchange rates between the two currencies are fixed by the monetary authorities under the rules framed by the International Monetary Fund. All payments for imports are to be made in the exporting country's currency which is not freely available in importers country. The scarcity of foreign currency may sometimes limit the size of imports from other countries.

5. Tariffs and Quotas

The tariff rates and quotas imposed by various countries on their exports and imports do not directly and significantly influence domestic business operations. The international businesses are directly and significantly influenced by the tariff rates imposed by various countries. Also they have to operate within the quotas of exports and imports imposed by different countries.

6. Research and Development

It is reasonable and relatively simpler to carry out business product research, innovations, demand analysis and customer survey in domestic business. Also the reliability and success rate of their results are much higher.

7. Human Resources

Due to past successes, proven track record and established systems, business can prosper even if the human resources have minimum skills and knowledge. The task of human resources management is much simpler in domestic business.

8. Organizational Vision and Objective

The organizational vision and objective in domestic business is narrowed down to work in a single country with a steady growth objective.

9. Investment

Depending on the size of domestic business operations one can start with a minimum investment. Involvement of regulatory bodies in respect of small local business enterprises is limited. On the other hand all overseas operations except exports, call for huge investments to set up and expand the business in many countries. Special regulatory bodies are involved in the process since foreign currency is transacted.

10. Distribution

Domestic business houses can use at its discretion to select any distribution channel to reach the customer. The choice of distribution channel in international business operations is governed by the government or market practice of the nation where the business is operating.

11. Logistics

Domestic business may involve use of conventional logistical methods engaging domestic players for procurement of raw materials and reaching of final products to the consumer.

12. Advertising and Promotion

Advertising, personal selling and other promotional methods are subject to the regulations prevailing in the domestic business operations.

13. Difference in Natural and Geographical Conditions

Natural resources like availability of raw materials, composition of soil, fertility of soil, rainfall, temperature etc. differ widely from country to country. On the basis of this specialty, countries specialise themselves in the production of certain selected commodities and therefore they produce better quality of goods at lower rates and sell them in the international market. It causes difference in domestic trade and foreign trade.

14. Different Legal Systems

Different legal systems are operated by different countries and they all widely differ from each other. The existence of different legal systems makes the task of businessmen more difficult as they have to follow legal provisions of the two countries as regards the particular trade.

15. Mobility of Factors of Production

Mobility of different factors of production is less as between nations 8 PP-IB&LP than in the country itself. However, with the advent of air transport, the mobility of labour has increased manifold. Similarly mobility of capital has increased with the development of international banking. In spite of these developments, mobility of labour and capital is not as much as it is found within the country itself.

17. Sovereign Political Entities

Each country is an independent sovereign political entity. Different countries impose different types of restrictions on imports and exports in the national interest. The importers and exporters shall have to observe such restrictions while entering into agreement.

Balance of Trade

The difference in value over a period of time between a country's imports and exports of goods and services. The balance of trade, commercial balance, or net exports is the difference between the monetary value of a nation's exports and imports over a certain period.

Factors Affecting the Balance of Trade

1) Impact of Inflation

If a country's inflation rate increases relative to the countries with which it trades, its current account will be expected to decrease, other things being equal. Consumers and corporations in that country will most likely purchases more goods overseas (due to high local inflations), while the country's exports to other countries will decline.

2) Impact of National Income

If a country's income level (national income) increases by a higher percentage than those of other countries, its current account is expected to decrease, other things being equal. As the real income level (adjusted for inflation) rises, so does consumption of goods. A percentage of that increase in consumption will most likely reflect an increased demand for foreign goods.

3) Impact of Government Policies

A country's government can have a major effect on its balance of trade due to its policies on subsidizing exporters, restrictions on imports, or lack of enforcement on piracy.

4) Subsidies for Exporters

Some governments offer subsidies to their domestic firms, so that those firms can produce products at a lower cost than their global competitors. Thus, the demand for the exports produced by those firms is higher as a result of subsidies.

Many firms in China commonly receive free loans or free land from the government. These firms incur a lower cost of operations and are able to price their products lower as a result, which enables them to capture a larger share of the global market.

5) Restrictions on Imports

If a country's government imposes a tax on imported goods (often referred to as a tariff), the prices of foreign goods to consumers are effectively increased. Some industries, however, are more highly protected by tariffs than others. American apparel products and farm products have historically received more protection against foreign competition through high tariffs on related imports. In addition to tariffs, a government can reduce its country's imports by enforcing a quota, or a maximum limit that can be imported. Quotas have been commonly applied to a variety of goods imported by the United States and other countries.

6) Lack of Restrictions on Piracy

In some cases, a government can affect international trade flows by its lack of restrictions on piracy. In China, piracy is very common; individuals (called pirates) manufacture CDs and DVDs that look almost exactly like the original product produced in the United States and other countries. They sell the CDs and DVDs on the street at a price that is lower than the original product. They even sell the CDs and DVDs to retail stores. It has been estimated that U.S. producers of film, music, and software lose $2 billion in sales per year due to piracy in China.

7) Impact of Exchange Rates

Each country's currency is valued in terms of other currencies through the use of exchange rates, so. that currencies can be exchanged to facilitate international transactions.

Balance of Payments: Meaning

The Balance of Payment (BOP) of a country is a systematic account of all economic transactions between a country and the rest of the world, undertaken during a specific period of time. BOP is the difference between all receipts from foreign countries and all payments to foreign countries. If the receipts exceed payments, then a country is said to have favourable BOP, and vice versa.

According to Charles Kindle Berger "The BOP of a country is a systematic recording of all economic transactions between residents of that country and the rest of the world during a given period of time".

The Balance of payments record is maintained in a standard double - entry book - keeping method. International transactions enter into record as credit or debit. The payments received from foreign countries enter as credit and payments made to other countries as debit.

Components of Balance of Payments

The three main components of BoP:

a)   Current Account

b)   Capital Account

c)   Official Reserve Transactions

The current account includes all the transactions related *to export and import of goods and services, investment income, and unilateral transfers (remittances, gifts, grants etc.).* The capital account includes all international asset transactions (FDI, FPI etc.). The official reserve transactions are conducted by central banks like RBI whenever there is BoP deficit or BoP surplus. These transactions are conducted in the form of international reserve assets, such as gold and major international currencies. The sum of the three BoP components should be zero. There is another element in BoP that is 'Errors and Omissions', which is the balancing item reflecting our inability to record all international transactions accurately.

BoP = Current Account + Capital Account + Official Reserve Transactions + Errors and Omissions = 0

Generally, when the joint of sum of current account and capital account of BoP is negative, it is referred as 'BoP deficit'. When the term 'BoP deficit' is used, we leave aside the official reserve transactions. Similarly, 'BoP surplus' means there is surplus in the joint sum of current account and capital account of BoP. Whenever we use the terms BoP Equilibrium and BoP Disequilibrium, we consider only current account and capital account.

Balance of Payments Account

Receipts (Credits)	**Payments (Debits)**
1. Export of goods.	Imports of goods.

Trade Account Balance

2. Export of services.	Import of services.
3. Interest, profit and dividends received.	Interest, profit and dividends paid.
4. Unilateral receipts.	Unilateral payments.

Current Account Balance (1 to 4)

5. Foreign investments.	Investments abroad.
6. Short term borrowings.	Short term lending.
7. Medium and long term Borrowing.	Medium and long term lending.

Capital Account Balance (5 to 7)

8. Errors and omissions.	Errors and omissions.
9. Change in reserves. (+)	Change in reserve (-)

Total Reciepts   =   Total Payments

Factors Affecting Balance of Payments

1. The Prevailing Exchange Rate of the Domestic Currency

A lower value of the domestic currency results in the domestic price getting translated into a lower international price. This increases the demand for domestic goods and services and hence their export. This is likely to result in a higher demand for the domestic currency. A higher exchange rate would have an exactly opposite effect.

2. Inflation Rate

The inflation rate in an economy vis-à-vis other economies affects the international competitiveness of the domestic goods and hence their demand. Higher the inflation, lower the competitiveness and lower the demand for domestic goods. Yet, a lower demand for domestic goods and services need not necessarily mean a lower demand for the domestic currency. If the demand for domestic goods is relatively inelastic, then the fall in demand may not offset the rise in price completely, resulting in an increase in the value of exports. This would end up increasing the demand for the local currency. For example, suppose India exports 100 quintals of wheat to the US at a price of Rs.500 per quintal. Further, assume that due to domestic inflation, the price increases to Rs.530 per quintal and there is a resultant fall in the quantity demanded to 96 quintals. The exports would increase fromRs.50,000 to Rs.52,800 instead of falling.

3. World Prices of a Commodity

If the price of a commodity increases in the world market, the value of exports for that particular product shows a corresponding increase. This would result in an increase in the demand for the domestic currency. A fall in the demand for domestic currency would be experienced in case of a reduction in the international price of a commodity. This impact is different from the previous one. The previous example considered an increase in the domestic prices of all goods produced in an economy simultaneously, while this one considers a change in the international price of a single commodity due to some exogenous reasons.

4. Incomes of Foreigners

There is a positive correlation between the incomes of there residents of an economy to which the domestic goods are exported, and exports. Hence, other things remaining the same, an increase in the standard of living (and hence, an increase in the incomes of the residents) of such an economy will result in an increase in the exports of the domestic economy Once again, this would increase the demand for the local currency.

5. Trade Barriers

Higher the trade barriers erected by other economies against the exports from a country, lower will be the demand for its exports a hence, for its currency.

6. Imports of Goods and Services

Imports of goods and services are affected by the same factors that affect the exports. While some factors have the same effect on imports as on exports, so of them have an exactly opposite effect.

7. Value of the Domestic Currency

An appreciation of the domestic currency results in making imported goods and services cheaper in terms of domestic currency which increasing their demand. The increased demand imports results in an increased supply of the domestic currency depreciation of the domestic currency have an opposite effect.

8. Level of Domestic Income

An increase in the level of domestic income increases the demand for all goods and services, including imports and it results in an increased supply of the domestic currency.

9. International Prices

The International demand and supply positions deter the international price of a commodity. A higher international price would translate into a higher domestic price. If the demand for imported goods is inelastic, this would result in a higher domestic currency value of in increasing the supply of the domestic currency. In case of the demand elastic, the effect on the supply of the domestic currency would depend the effect on the domestic currency value of imports.

10. Inflation Rate

A domestic inflation rate that is higher than the inflation of other economies, would result in imported goods and services bee relatively cheaper than domestically produced goods and services would increase the demand for the former, and hence, the supply domestic currency.

11. Income on Investments

Both payments and receipts on account of interest, dividends, profits etc., depend on the level of past investments and the current rates of return that can be earned in an economy. For payments, it is the level of past foreign investments and the current domestic rates of return;

while for the receipts it is the past domestic investments in foreign economies and the current foreign rates of return, which are relevant.

12. Transfer Payments

Transfer payments are broadly affected by two factors. One is the number of migrants to or from a country, who may receive money from or send money to relatives. The second is the desire of a country to generate goodwill by granting aids to other countries along with the economic capability to do so, or its need to take aids and grants from other countries to tide over difficulties.

13. Capital Account Transactions

Four major factors affect international capital transactions. The foremost is the rate of return which can be earned on the investments as compared to the returns that can be earned on domestic investments. The higher the differential returns offered by a country, the higher will be the capital inflows. Another factor is the additional risk that accompanies these returns. More the risk, lower the capital inflows. Diversification across countries may offer some extra benefit in addition to the returns offered by a particular investment. This benefit arises from the fact that different economies may be at different stages of economic cycle at a given time, thus making their performance unrelated. Higher the diversification benefits, higher the inflows. One more factor, which has a very significant affect on these transactions, is the expected movement in the exchange rates. If the exchange rates are quite stable, or the movement is expected to be in the investors' favor, the capital inflows will be higher

Equilibrium and Disequilibrium in Balance of Payments

Balance of payments is the difference between the receipts from and payments to foreigners by residents of a country. In accounting sense balance of payments, must always balance. Debits must be equal to credits. So, there will be equilibrium in balance of payments.

$$\text{Symbolically, } B = R - P$$

Where:

B = Balance of Payments

R = Receipts from Foreigners

P = Payments made to Foreigners

When B = Zero, there is said to be equilibrium in balance of payments.

When B is positive there is favourable balance of payments; When &. B is negative there is unfavorable or adverse balance of payments.' When there is a surplus or a deficit in balance of payments there is said : to be disequilibrium in balance of payments. Thus disequilibrium refers to imbalance in balance of payments.

Types of Disequilibrium in BOP

The following are the main types of disequilibrium in the balance of payments:-

1. Structural Disequilibrium:

Structural disequilibrium is caused by structural changes in the economy affecting demand and Supply relations in commodity and factor markets. Some of the structural disequilibrium are as follows:

- A shift in demand due to changes in tastes, fashions, income etc. would decrease or increase the demand for imported goods thereby causing a disequilibrium in BOP.
- If foreign demand for a country's products declines due to new and cheaper substitutes abroad, then the country's exports will decline causing a deficit.
- Changes in the rate of international capital movements may also cause structural disequilibrium.
- If supply is affected due to crop failure, shortage of raw-materials, strikes, political instability etc.,
- then there would be deficit in BOP.
- A war or natural calamities also result in structural changes which may affect not only goods but also factors of production causing disequilibrium in BOP.
- Institutional changes that take place within and outside the country may result in BOP disequilibrium. For Eg. if a trading block imposes additional import duties on products imported in member countries of the block, then the exports of exporting country would be restricted or reduced. This may worsen the BOP position of exporting country.

2. Cyclical Disequilibrium

Economic activities are subject to business cycles, which normally have four phases Boom or Prosperity, Recession, Depression and Recovery. During boom period, imports may increase considerably due to increase in demand for imported goods. During recession and depression, imports may be reduced due to fall in demand on account of reduced income. During recession exports may increase due to fall in prices. During boom period, a country may face deficit in BOP on account of increased imports. Cyclical disequilibrium in BOP may occur because

- Trade cycles follow different paths and patterns in different countries.
- Income elasticities of demand for imports in different countries are not identical.
- Price elasticities of demand for imports differ in different countries.

3. Short - Run Disequilibrium

This disequilibrium occurs for a short period of one or two years. Such BOP disequilibrium is temporary in nature. Short - run disequilibrium arises due to unexpected contingencies like failure of rains or favourable monsoons, strikes, industrial peace or unrest etc. Imports may increase exports or exports may increase imports in a year due to these reasons and causes a temporary disequilibrium exists.

International borrowing or lending for a short-period would cause short-run disequilibrium in balance of payments of a country. Short term disequilibrium can be corrected through short-term borrowings. If short - run disequilibrium occurs repeatedly it may pave way for long-run disequilibrium.

4. Long - Run I Secular Disequilibrium

Long run or fundamental disequilibrium refers to a persistent deficit or a surplus in the balance of payments of a country. It is also known as secular disequilibrium. The causes of long – term disequilibrium are

- Continuous increase in demand for imports due to increasing population.
- Constant price changes - mostly inflation which affects exports on continuous basis.
- Decline in demand for exports due to technological improvements in importing countries, and as such the importing countries depend less on imports.

The long run disequilibrium can be corrected by making constant efforts to increase exports and to reduce imports.

5. Monetary Disequilibrium

Monetary disequilibrium takes place on account of inflation or deflation. Due to inflation, prices of products in domestic market rises, which makes exports expensive. Such a situation may affect BOP equilibrium. Inflation also results in increase in money income with people, which in turn may increase demand for imported goods. As a result imports may turn BOP position in disequilibrium.

6. Exchange Rate Fluctuations

A high degree of fluctuation in exchange rate may affect the BOP position. For Eg. if Indian Rupee gets appreciated against dollar, then Indian exporters will receive lower amounts of foreign exchange, whereas, there will be more outflow of foreign exchange on account of higher imports. Such a situation will adversely affect BOP position. But, if domestic currency depreciates against foreign currency, then the BOP position may have positive impact.

Main Causes of BOP Disequilibrium

Any disequilibrium in the balance of payment is the result of imbalance between receipts and payments for imports and exports. Normally, the term disequilibrium is interpreted from a negative angle and therefore, it implies deficit in BOP. The disequilibrium in BOP is caused due to various factors.

I Import - Related Causes

The rise in imports has been the most important factor responsible for large BOP deficits. The causes of rapid expansion of imports are :-

1. Population Growth

Population Growth may increase the demand for imported goods such as food items and non food items, to meet their growing needs. Thus, increase in imports may lead to BOP disequilibrium.

2. Development Programme

Increase in development programmes by developing countries may require import of capital goods, raw materials and technology. As development is a continuous process, imports of these items continue for a long time landing the developing countries in BOP deficit.

3 Imports of Essential Items

Countries which do not have enough supply of essential items like Crude oil or Capital equipments are required to import them. Again due to natural calamities government may resort to heavy imports, which adversely affect the BOP position.

4. Reduction of Import Duties

When import duties are reduced, imports becomes cheaper as such imports increases. This increases the deficit in BOP position.

5. Inflation

Inflation in domestic markets may increase the demand for imported goods, provided the imported goods are available at lower prices than in domestic markets.

6. Demonstration Effect

An increase in income coupled with awareness of higher living standard of foreigners, induce people at home to imitate the foreigners. When people become victims of demonstration effect, their propensity to import would increases.

II. Export Related Causes

Even though export earnings have increased but they have not been sufficient enough to meet the rising imports. Exports may reduce without a corresponding decline in imports. Following are the causes for decrease in exports

1. Increase in Population

Goods which were earlier exported may be consumed by rising population. This reduces the export earnings of the country leading to BOP disequilibrium.

2. Inflation

When there is inflation in domestic market, prices of export goods increases. This reduces the demand of export goods which in turn results in trade deficit.

3. Appreciation of Currency

Appreciation of domestic currency against foreign currencies results in lower foreign exchange to exporters. This demotivates the exporters.

4. Discovery of Substitutes

With technological development new substitutes have come up. Like plastic for rubber, synthetic fiber for cotton etc. This may reduce the demand for raw material requirement.

5. Technological Development

Technological Development in importing countries may reduce their imports. This can be possible when they start manufacturing goods which they were exporting earlier. This will have an adverse effect on exporting countries.

6. Protectionist Trade Policy

Protectionist trade policy of importing country would encourage domestic producers by giving them incentives, whereas, the imports would be discouraged by imposing high duties. This will affect exports.

III Other Causes

1. Flight of Capital

Due to speculative reasons, countries may lose foreign exchange or gold stocks. Investors may also withdraw their investments, which in turn put pressure on foreign exchange reserves.

2. Globalisation

Globalisation and the rules of WTO have brought a liberal and open environment in global trade. It has positive as well as negative effects on imports, exports and investments.

Poor countries are unable to cope up with this new environment. Ultimately they become loser and their BOP is adversely affected.

3. Cyclical Transmission

International trade is also affected by Business cycles. Recession or depression in one or more developed countries may affect the rest of the world. The negative effects of trade cycle (low income, low demand, etc.) are transmitted from one country to another.

4. Structural Adjustments

Many countries in recent years are undergoing structural changes. Their economies are being liberalised. As a result, investment, income and other variables are changing resulting in changes in exports and imports.

5. Political Factors

The existence of political instability may result in disrupting the productive apparatus of the country causing a decline in exports and increase in imports.

Likewise, payment of war expenses may also serious affect disequilibrium in the country's BOP. Thus political factors may also produce serious disequilibrium in the country's BOPs.

Measures to Correct Disequilibrium in BOP

Any disequilibrium (deficit or surplus) in balance of payments is bad for normal internal economic operations and international economic relations. A deficit is more harmful for a country's economic growth, thus it must be corrected sooner than later.

The measures to correct disequilibrium can be broadly divided into four groups

I. Monetary Measures

1) Monetary Policy

The monetary policy is concerned with money supply and credit in the economy. The Central Bank may expand or contract the money supply in the economy through appropriate measures which will affect the prices.

A. Inflation

If in the country there is inflation, the Central Bank through its monetary policy will make an attempt to reduce inflation. The Central Bank will adopt tight monetary policy. Money supply will be controlled by increase in Bank Rate, Cash Reserve Ratio, Statutory Ratio etc.

The monetary policy measures may reduce money supply, and encourage people to save more, which would reduce inflation. If inflation is reduced, the prices of domestic market will decrease and also that of export goods. In foreign markets there will be more demand for export goods, which would correct BOP disequilibrium.

B. Deflation

During deflation the Central Bank of the country may adopt easy monetary policy. It will try to increase money supply and credit in the economy, which would increase investment. More investment leads to more production. Surplus can be exported, which in turn may improve BOP position.

2) Fiscal Policy

Fiscal policy is government's policy on income and expenditure. Government incurs development and non - development expenditure,. It gets income through taxation and non - tax sources. Depending upon the situation government's expenditure may be increased or decreased.

a) Inflation

During inflation the government may adopt easy fiscal policy. The tax rates for corporate sector may be reduced, which would encourage more production and distribution including exports. Increased exports will bring more foreign exchange there by making the BOP position favourable.

b) Deflation

During deflation the government would adopt restrictive fiscal policy. It may impose additional taxes on consumers or may introduce tax saving schemes. This may reduce the consumption of citizens, which in turn may enable more export surplus. To restrict imports the government may also impose additional tariffs or customs duties which may improve the BOP position.

3) Exchange Rate Policy

Foreign exchange rate in the market may directly or indirectly be influenced by the Government.

a) Devaluation

When foreign exchange problem is faced by the country, the government tries to reduce imports and .increase exports. This is done through devaluation of domestic currency. Under devaluation, the- government makes a deliberate effort to reduce the value of home country. If devaluation is carried out, then the exports will become cheaper and imports costlier. This is turn will help to reduce imports and increase exports.

b) Depreciation

Depreciation like devaluation lowers the value of domestic currency or increases the value of foreign currency. Depreciation of a country's currency takes place in free or competitive foreign exchange market due to market forces.

Depreciation and devaluation have the same effect on exchange rate. If there is high demand for foreign currency than its supply, it will appreciate and vice versa. However, in several countries the system of managed flexibility is followed. If there is more demand for foreign exchange, the central bank will release the foreign currency in the market from its reserves so as to reduce the appreciation of foreign currency. If there is less demand for foreign exchange, it will purchase the foreign currency from market so as to reduce the depreciation of foreign country and appreciation of domestic currency. Due to devaluation and depreciation of domestic currency, the exports become cheaper and imports become expensive. This helps to increase exports.

II) Non-Monetary/General Measures

A deficit country along with monetary measures may adopt the following non-monetary measures too, which will either restrict imports or promote exports.

1) Tariffs

Tariffs refer to duties on imports to restrict imports. Tariff is a fiscal device which may be used to correct an adverse balance of payments. The imposition of import duties will raise the prices of imports. This will lead to a reduction in demand for imports thereby improving the balance of payments position.

2) Quotas

Under Quota System, the government may fix and permit the maximum quantity or value of a commodity to be imported during a given period. By restricting imports through quota system, the deficit is reduced and the balance of payments position is improved.

3) Export Promotion

The government may introduce a number of export promotion measures to encourage exporters to export more so as to earn valuable foreign exchange, which in turn would improve BOP Situation. Some of the incentives are Subsidies, Tax Concessions, Grants, Octroi refund, Excise exemption, Duty Drawback, Marketing facilities etc.

4) Import Substitution

Governments, especially, that of the developing countries may encourage import substitution so as to restrict imports and save valuable foreign exchange. The government may encourage domestic producers to produce goods which were earlier imported. The domestic producers may be given several incentives such as Tax holiday, Cash Subsidy, Assistance in Research & Development, Providing technical assistance, Providing Scarce inputs etc. From the above measures it is clear that more exports with import substitution based on economic strength of the country are the real effective solutions to correct the disequilibrium in the balance of payments.

Balance of Trade Vs Balance of Payments

1. Balance of trade is the difference between the values of a country's total imports and exports of goods and services. Balance of trade appears under the current account of the balance of payments. Balance of payments records all of the country's transactions and inflows and outflows of funds between the local economy and foreign economies.

2. The balance of trade is narrower in scope as it does not take into consideration capital and financial transactions. The balance of payments, on the other hand, is more comprehensive as it covers all international transactions.

3. The balance of trade is a component of the balance of payments and is recorded under one of the main components of the balance of payments; the current account.

4. The balance of trade shows only the difference between the value of a country's total imports and exports of goods and services,. The balance of payments shows an overall view of the country's financial status by taking into consideration transfers of capital, transfers of assets and funds, international investments, sales and purchases of assets, remittances, gifts, unilateral transfers, changes in reserves, etc.

5. The balance of trade (BOT) is a component in the balance of payment which makes up a large part of the current account. Balance of payments (BOP) records a country's total inflows and outflows of funds and assets to and from foreign countries and offers an overview of all international monetary transactions. The balance of payments provides a summary of all transactions during the year and offers a clear snapshot of the country's financial status.

Exim Policy

Exim Policy, also known as the Foreign Trade Policy is announced every 5 years by Ministry of Commerce and Industry, Government of India. It is updated every year on the 31st of March and all the amendments and improvements in the scheme are effective from the 1st of April. Exim policy deals in general provisions pertaining to exports and imports, promotional measures, duty exemption schemes, export promotion schemes, special economic zone programs and other details for different sectors. The Government announces a supplement to this policy each year. EXIM policy refers to the policy measures adopted by a country with reference to its exports and imports.

Objectives of the Exim Policy

The main objective of the Government's EXIM Policy is to promote exports to the maximum extent. Exports should be promoted in such a manner that the economy of the country is not affected by unregulated exportable items specially needed within the country. Export control is, therefore, exercised in respect of a limited number of items whose supply position demands that their exports should be regulated in the larger interests of the country. In other words, the main objectives of the Exim Policy are:

1. To accelerate the economy from low level of economic activities to high level of economic activities by making it a globally oriented vibrant economy and to derive maximum benefits from expanding global market opportunities.
2. To stimulate sustained economic growth by providing access to essential raw materials, intermediates, components,' consumables and capital goods required for augmenting production.
3. To enhance the techno local strength and efficiency of Indian agriculture, industry and services, thereby, improving their competitiveness.
4. To generate new employment.
5. Opportunities and encourage the attainment of internationally accepted standards of quality.
6. To provide quality consumer products at reasonable prices.

Exim Policy 2015-2020

The Government of India, Ministry of Commerce and Industry announced New Foreign Trade Policy on 1st April 2015 for the period 2015-2020, earlier this policy known as Export Import (Exim) Policy. After five years foreign trade policy needs amendments in general, aims at developing export potential, improving export performance, encouraging foreign trade and creating favorable balance of payments position. The Export Import Policy (EXIM Policy) or Foreign Trade Policy is updated every year on the 31st of March and the modifications, improvements and new schemes becomes effective from April month of each year.

Highlights of Exim Policy 2015-2020

A. Export from India Schemes

1. Merchandise Exports from India Scheme (MEIS)

Earlier there were 5 different schemes (Focus Product Scheme, Market Linked Focus Product Scheme, Focus Market Scheme, Agriculture Infrastructure Incentive Scrip, VKGUY) for rewarding merchandise exports with different kinds of duty scrips with varying conditions (sector specific or actual user only) attached to their use. Now all these schemes have been merged into a single scheme, namely Merchandise Export from India Scheme (MEIS) and there would be no conditionality attached to the scrips issued under the scheme.

Rewards for export of notified goods to notified markets under 'Merchandise Exports from India Scheme (MEIS) shall be payable as percentage of realized FOB value (in free foreign exchange). The debits towards basic customs duty in the transferable reward duty credit scrips would also be allowed adjustment as duty drawback. At present, only the additional duty of customs / excise duty / service tax is allowed adjustment as CENVAT credit or drawback, as per Department of Revenue rules.

2. Service Exports from India Scheme (SEIS)

Served From India Scheme (SFIS) has been replaced with Service Exports from India Scheme (SEIS). SEIS shall apply to 'Service Providers located in India' instead of 'Indian Service Providers'. Thus SEIS provides for rewards to all Service providers of notified services, who are providing services from India, regardless of the constitution or profile of the service provider.

The rate of reward under SEIS would be based on net foreign exchange earned. The reward issued as duty credit scrip, would no longer be with actual user condition and will no longer be restricted to usage for specified types of goods but be freely transferable and usable for all types of goods and service tax debits on procurement of services / goods. Debits would be eligible for CENVAT credit or drawback.

3. Incentives (MEIS & SEIS) to be available for Special Economic Zones

It is now proposed to extend Incentives (MEIS & SEIS) to units located in SEZs also.

4. Duty credit Scrips to be freely transferable and usable for payment of custom duty, excise duty and service tax

All scrips issued under MEIS and SEIS and the goods imported against these scrips would be fully transferable. Scrips issued under Exports from India Schemes can be used for the following:

1. Payment of customs duty for import of inputs / goods including capital goods, except items listed in Appendix 3A.
2. Payment of excise duty on domestic procurement of inputs or goods, including capital goods.
3. Payment of service tax on procurement of services.

Basic Customs Duty paid in cash or through debit under Duty Credit Scrip can be taken back as Duty Drawback as per Department of Revenue Rules, if inputs so imported are used for exports.

5. Status Holders

Business leaders who have excelled in international trade and have successfully contributed to country's foreign trade are proposed to be recognized as Status Holders and given special treatment and privileges to facilitate their trade transactions, in order to reduce their transaction costs and time.

The nomenclature of Export House, Star Export House, Trading House, Star Trading House, Premier Trading House certificate has been changed to One, Two, Three, Four, Five Star Export House. The criteria for export performance for recognition of status holder have been changed from Rupees to US dollar earnings.

B. Boost to "Make in India"

With the objective of making the country a manufacturing hub for domestic and foreign companies, Prime Minister Narendra Modi launched the NDA Government's "Make in India" campaign rolling out a red carpet to attract industrialists to make India a global manufacturing hub, to help create jobs and boost economic growth.. The "Make in India" initiative will act as a first reference point for guiding foreign investors on all aspects of regulatory and policy issues and assist them in obtaining regulatory clearances. The Centre has already allowed 100% Foreign Direct Investment (FDI) under the automatic route in construction, operation and maintenance in rail infrastructure projects and increased FDI in defence from 26 to 49 per cent.

1.   Reduced Export Obligation for domestic procurement under EPCG scheme: Specific Export Obligation under EPCG scheme, in case capital goods are procured from indigenous manufacturers, which is currently 90% of the normal export obligation (6 times at the duty saved amount) has been reduced to 75%, in order to promote domestic capital goods manufacturing industry.

2. Higher level of rewards under MEIS for export items with high domestic content and value addition.

It is proposed to give higher level of rewards to products with high domestic content and value addition, as compared to products with high import content and less value addition.

C. Trade Facilitation & Ease of Doing Business

1. Online Filing of Documents/ Applications and Paperless Trade in 24x7 Environments

DGFT already provides facility of Online filing of various applications under FTP by the exporters/ importers. However, certain documents like Certificates issued by Chartered Accountants/ Company Secretary / Cost Accountant etc. have to be filed in physical forms only. In order to move further towards paperless processing of reward schemes, it has been decided to develop an online procedure to upload digitally signed documents by Chartered Accountant / Company Secretary / Cost Accountant. In the new system, it will be possible to upload online documents like annexure attached to ANF 3B, ANF 3C and ANF 3D, which are at present signed by these signatories and submitted physically.

Henceforth, hardcopies of applications and specified documents would not be required to be submitted. As a measure of ease of doing business, landing documents of export consignment as proofs for notified market can be digitally uploaded in the following manner:-

- Any exporter may upload the scanned copy of Bill of Entry under his digital signature.
- Status holders falling in the category of Three Star, Four Star or Five Star Export House may upload scanned copies of documents.

2. Online Inter-ministerial Consultations

It is proposed to have Online inter-ministerial consultations for approval of export of SCOMET items, Norms fixation, Import Authorisation, Export Authorisation, in a phased manner, with the objective to reduce time for approval. As a result, there would not be any need to submit hard copies of documents for these purposes by the exporters.

3. Simplification of Procedures/Processes, Digitization and e-governance

Under EPCG scheme, obtaining and submitting a certificate from an independent Chartered Engineer, confirming the use of spares, tools, refractory and catalysts imported for final redemption of EPCG authorizations has been dispensed with.

At present, the EPCG Authorisation holders are required to maintain records for 3 years after redemption of Authorisation. Now the EPCG Authorization Holders shall be required to maintain records for a period of two years only. Government's endeavour is to gradually phase out this requirement as the relevant records such as Shipping Bills, e-BRC are likely to be available in electronic mode which can be archived and retrieved whenever required.

Exporter Importer Profile: Facility has been created to upload documents in Exporter/ Importer Profile. There will be no need to submit copies of permanent records/ documents (e.g. IEC, Manufacturing licence, RCMC, PAN etc.) repeatedly with each application, once uploaded.

Communication with Exporters/Importers: Certain information, like mobile number, e-mail address etc. has been added as mandatory fields, in IEC data base. This information once provided by exporters, would help in better communication with exporters. SMS/ email would be sent to exporters to inform them about issuance of authorisations or status of their applications.

Online message exchange with CBDT and MCA: It has been decided to have on line message exchange with CBDT for PAN data and with Ministry of Corporate Affairs for CIN and DIN data. This integration would obviate the need for seeking information from IEC holders for subsequent amendments/ updating of data in IEC data base.

Communication with Committees of DGFT: For faster and paperless communication with various committees of DGFT, dedicated e-mail addresses have been provided to each Norms Committee, Import Committee and Pre-Shipment Inspection Agency for faster communication.

Online applications for refunds: Online filing of application for refund of TED is being introduced for which a new ANF has been created.

4. Forthcoming e-Governance Initiatives

(a) DGFT is Currently Working on the following EDI Initiatives

  i.   Message exchange for transmission of export reward scrips from DGFT to Customs.
  ii.   Message exchange for transmission of Bills of Entry (import details) from Customs to DGFT.
  iii. Online issuance of Export Obligation Discharge Certificate.

iv.   Message exchange with Ministry of Corporate Affairs for CIN & DIN.

v.   Message exchange with CBDT for PAN.

vi.   Facility to pay application fee using debit card / credit card.

vii.   Open API for submission of IEC application.

viii.   Mobile applications for FTP

D. Other New Initiatives

1. New Initiatives for EOUs, EHTPs and STPs

EOUs, EHTPs, STPs have been allowed to share infrastructural facilities among themselves. This will enable units to utilize their infrastructural facilities in an optimum way and avoid duplication of efforts and cost to create separate infrastructural facilities in different units.

Inter unit transfer of goods and services have been allowed among EOUs, EHTPs, STPs, and BTPs. This will facilitate group of those units which source inputs centrally in order to obtain bulk discount. This will reduce cost of transportation, other logistic costs and result in maintaining effective supply chain.

EOUs have been allowed facility to set up Warehouses near the port of export. This will help in reducing lead time for delivery of goods and will also address the issue of un-predictability of supply orders.

STP units, EHTP units, software EOUs have been allowed the facility to use all duty free equipment/ goods for training purposes. This will help these units in developing skills of their employees.

100% EOU units have been allowed facility of supply of spares/ components up to 2% of the value of the manufactured articles to a buyer in domestic market for the purpose of after sale services.

At present, in a period of 5 years EOU units have to achieve Positive Net Foreign Exchange Earning (NEE) cumulatively. Because of adverse market condition or any ground of genuine hardship, then such period of 5 years for NFE completion can be extended by one year.

Time period for validity of Letter of Permission (LOP) for EOUs/EHTP/ STPI/BTP Units has been revised for faster implementation and monitoring of projects. Now, LOP will have an initial validity of 2 years to enable the unit to construct the plant and install the machinery. Further extension can be granted by the Development Commissioner up to one year. Extensions beyond 3 years of the validity of LOP, can be granted, in case unit has completed 2/3rd of activities, including the construction activities.

At present, EOUs/EHTP/STPI units are permitted to transfer capital goods to other EOUs, EHTPs, STPs, SEZ units. Now a facility has been provided that if such transferred capital goods are rejected by the recipient, then the same can be returned to the supplying unit, without payment of duty.

A simplified procedure will be provided to fast track the de-bonding / exit of the STP/ EHTP units. This will save time for these units and help in reduction of transaction cost.

EOUs having physical export turnover of Rs.10 crores and above, have been allowed the facility of fast track clearances of import and domestic procurement. They will be allowed fast tract clearances of goods, for export production, on the basis of pre-authenticated procurement certificate, issued by customs/central excise authorities. They will not have to seek procurement permission for every import consignment.

2. Facilitating & Encouraging Export of Dual Use Items (SCOMET)

Validity of SCOMET export Authorisation has been extended from the present 12 months to 24 months. It will help industry to plan their activity in an orderly manner and obviate the need to seek revalidation or relaxation from DGFT.

- Authorisation for repeat orders will be considered on automatic basis subject to certain conditions.
- Verification of End User Certificate (EUC) is being simplified if SCOMET item is being exported under Defence Export Offset Policy.
- Outreach programmes will be conducted at different locations to raise awareness among various stakeholders.

3. Facilitating & Encouraging Export of Defence Exports

Normal export obligation period under advance authorization is 18 months. Export obligation period for export items falling in the category of defence, military store, aerospace and nuclear energy shall be 24 months from the date of issue of authorization or co-terminus with contracted duration of the export order, whichever is later. This provision will help export of defence items and other high technology items.

A list of military stores requiring NOC of Department of Defence Production has been notified by DGFT recently. A committee has been formed to create ITC (HS) codes for defence and security items for which industrial licenses are issued by DIPP.

4. e-Commerce Exports

Goods falling in the category of handloom products, books / periodicals, leather footwear, toys and customized fashion garments, having FOB value up to Rs.25000 per consignment (finalized using e-Commerce platform) shall be eligible for benefits under FTP. Such goods can be exported in manual mode through Foreign Post Offices at New Delhi, Mumbai and Chennai.

Export of such goods under Courier Regulations shall be allowed manually on pilot basis through Airports at Delhi, Mumbai and Chennai as per appropriate amendments in regulations to be made by Department of Revenue. Department of Revenue shall fast track the implementation of EDI mode at courier terminals.

5. Duty Exemption

Imports against Advance Authorization shall also be eligible for exemption from Transitional Product Specific Safeguard Duty.

Order to encourage manufacturing of capital goods in India, import under EPCG Authorisation Scheme shall not be eligible for exemption from payment of anti-dumping duty, safeguard duty and transitional product specific safeguard duty.

6. Additional Ports allowed for Export and Import

Calicut Airport, Kerala and Arakonam, Tamil Nadu have been notified as registered ports for import and export.

7. Duty Free Tariff Preference Scheme

India has already extended duty free tariff preference to 33 Least Developed Countries across the globe. This is being notified under FTP.

8. Quality Complaints and Trade Disputes

In an endeavour to resolve quality complaints and trade disputes, between exporters and importers, a new chapter, namely, Chapter on Quality Complaints and Trade Disputes has been incorporated in the Foreign Trade Policy. For resolving such disputes at a faster pace, a Committee on Quality Complaints and Trade Disputes (CQCTD) is being constituted in 22 offices and would have members from EPCs/EICs.

9. Towns of Export Excellence

Government has already recognized 33 towns as export excellence towns. It has been decided to add Vishakhapatnam and Bhimavaram in Andhra Pradesh as towns of export excellence.

EXPORT PROMOTION INSTITUTIONS

The Government of India has set up several institutions whose main functions are to help an exporter in his work. It would be advisable for an exporter to acquaint with these institutions and the nature of help that they can provide so that the exporter can initially contact them and have a clear picture about the expected help from the organized sources. Ministry of Commerce and industry is the primary government agency responsible for evolving and directing foreign trade policy ad program, including commercial relations with other countries, various trade promotional measures and development and regulation of certain export- oriented industries. There are deliberative and consultative organizations to ensure that export problems are comprehensively dealt with after mutual discussions between the Government and the Industry. They are as under:

1. Export Promotion Councils
2. Commodity boards
3. The Marine Products Export Development Authority
4. Agricultural and processed Food Products Export Development Authority
5. The Indian Institute of Foreign Trade
6. Indian Trade Promotion Organisation (ITPO)
7. National Centre for Trade Information
8. Indian Institute Packaging (IIP)
9. Indian Council of Arbitration (ICA)
10. Federation of Indian Export Organisation (FIEO)
11. Board of Trade
12. Export Inspection Council
13. Export credit and Guarantee Corporation
14. Export-Import Bank

Export Promotion Councils

The EPCs are non-profit organisations registered under the Companies Act or the Societies Registration Act, as the case may be. The basic objective of Export Promotion Councils is to promote and develop the exports of the country. Each Council is responsible for the promotion of a particular group of products, projects and services. The main role of the EPCs is to project India's image abroad as a reliable supplier of high quality goods and services. In particular, the EPCs shall encourage and monitor the observance of international standards and specifications by exporters. The EPCs shall keep abreast of the trends and opportunities in international markets for goods and services and assist their members in taking advantage of such opportunities in order to expand and diversify exports. The EPCs shall be autonomous and regulate their own affairs. However, if the Central Government frames uniform bylaws for the constitution and/ or for the transaction of business for EPCs, they shall adopt the same with such modifications as Central Government may approve having regard to the special nature or functioning of such EPC. The EPCs shall be required to obtain the approval of the Central Government for participation in trade fairs, exhibitions etc and for sending sales teams/ delegations abroad. The Ministry of Commerce and Industry/Ministry of Textiles of the Government of India, as the case may be, would interact with the Managing Committee of the Council concerned, twice a year, once for approving their annual plans and budget and again for a mid-year appraisal and review of their performance. In order to give a boost and impetus to exports, it is imperative that the EPCs function as professional bodies. For this purpose, executives with a professional background in commerce, management and international marketing and having experience in government and industry should be brought into the EPCs.

Functions of Export Promotion Councils

1. Providing Information

To assist exporters to understand, interpret and implement the export policies and export assistance schemes of Government.

2. Providing Assistance

To provide assistance in export promotional activities such as external publicity, participation in fairs and exhibitions, promotion of exclusive exhibitions and trade fairs of specific products.

3. Collecting Data

To collect complete data on export growth, the problems faced by exporters, the specific help needed by the manufacturers and present the same to the Government in order to enable it to evolve appropriate export policies.

4. Acting as Liaison

The council carries out an effective liaison with industry and trade in order to identify the problems in export activities.

5. Sending Trade Delegations

The council would make all arrangements for sending trade delegations and study teams to one or more countries for promoting the export of specific products and to circulate the reports of specific products and diversifying to new products.

6. Opening Office Abroad

It opens offices abroad to help exporters in consolidating the existing exports and diversifying to new products.

7. Registering Authority

EPC would act as registering authority under the import policy for registered exporters and to help them in expanding overseas market for their products.

8. Motivating Exporters

It creates consciousness among exporters through seminars, discussion and to motivate them for export promotion.

9. Co-operation with EIC

The council provides co operation to the export inspection council on quality control and pre-shipment inspection of export goods.

10. Disposing Applications

It provides assistance to members for speedy disposal of export assistance applications

11. Offering Guidance

The EPC offers guidance to member on various matters like utilization of GSP, export finance, insurance of goods and joint ventures aboard.

12. Indicating Export Opportunities

It collects and supply market information to exporter and thereby to help them to take benefits to take benefits of export opportunities available abroad.

13. Settling Disputes

The council enables the member in settling their trade disputes through peaceful negotiations.

14. Solving Transport Problems

It helps members to resolve their transport problems.

15. Concessions

The council assist members in getting freight and other concessions for shipping conferences.

16. Issuing Certificate of Origin

It issue certificate of origin to Indian exporters certifying the origin of goods. The EPCs helps Indian exporters through these functions in direct or indirect ways. They provide various services to Indian exporting communities. Each EPC has its working committee which elected by the members.

Types of EPCs

At present there are 21 EPCs dealing with various commodities.

They are as under

1. Agricultural and Processed Food Products Export Development Authority.
2. Basic Chemicals, Pharmaceuticals and Cosmetics Export Promotion Council.
3. Cashew Export Promotion Council.
4. Cotton Textiles Export Promotion Council.
5. Council for Leather Exports.
6. Carpet Export Promotion Council.
7. Export Promotion Council for Handicrafts.
8. Apparel Export Promotion Council
9. Engineering Export Promotion Council
10. Electronics & Computer Software EP
11. Gem & Jewellery Export Promotion Council
12. The Indian Silk Export Promotion Council
13. Jute Manufacturers Development Council
14. The Plastics Export Promotion Council
15. Powerloom Development & Export Promotion Council
16. Project Exports Promotion Council of India
17. Services Export Promotion Council
18. The Sports Goods Export Promotion Council
19. Shellac & Forest Products Export Promotion Council
20. Synthetic & Rayon Textiles Export Promotion Council
21. Wool Industry Export Promotion Council

Export Promotion Schemes

After the economic reforms of 1991-92, liberalization of external trade, elimination of duties on imports of information technology products, relaxation of controls on both inward and outward investments and foreign exchange and the fiscal measures taken by the Government of India and the individual State Governments specifically for IT and ITES have been major contributory factors for the sector to flourish in India and for the country to be able to acquire a dominant position in offshore services in the world. The major fiscal incentives provided by the Government of India have been for the Export Oriented Units (EOU), Software Technology Parks (STP), and Special Economic Zones (SEZ).

Software Technology Parks (STP)

For the promotion of Software exports from the country, the Software Technology Parks of India was set up in 1991 as an Autonomous Society under the Department of Electronics and Information Technology. The services rendered by STPI for the Software exporting community have been statutory services, data communications servers, incubation facilities, training and value added services. STPI has played a key developmental role in the promotion of software exports with a special focus on SMEs and start up units. The STP Scheme which is a 100% export oriented scheme has been successful in fostering the growth of the software industry. The exports made by STP Units have grown over the years. The STP scheme allows software companies to set up operations in convenient and inexpensive locations and plan their investment and growth driven by business needs. Over 4000 units are registered under STP Scheme.

Benefits of STP schemes

1. Customs Duty Exemption in full on imports.
2. Central Excise Duty Exemption in full on indigenous procurement.
3. Central Sales Tax Reimbursement on indigenous purchase
4. All relevant equipment / goods including second hand equipment can be imported (except prohibited items).
5. Equipment can also be imported on loan basis/lease.
6. 100% FDI is permitted through automatic route.
7. Sales in the DTA up to 50% of the FOB value of exports permissible.
8. Use of computer imported for training permissible subject to certain conditions.
9. Depreciation on computers at accelerated rates up to 100% over 5 years is permissible.

Special Economic Zones Schemes

A SEZ is defined as a "specifically demarked duty-free enclave and shall deemed to be foreign territory (out of Customs jurisdiction) for the purpose of trade operations and duties and tariffs". In 2005, the Department of Commerce, Ministry of Commerce & Industry, Government of India has enacted the Special Economic Zone (SEZ) Act, with an objective of providing an internationally competitive and hassle free environment for exports. It provides drastic simplification of procedures and a single window clearance policy on matters relating to central and state governments. The scheme is ideal for bigger Industries and has a significant impact on future Exports and employment. The SEZ policy aims at creating competitive, convenient and integrated Zones offering World class infrastructure, utilities and services for globally oriented businesses.

Salient Features of SEZ Scheme are as under

1. Duty free import/domestic procurement of goods for development, operation and maintenance of SEZ units.
2. 100% Income Tax exemption on export profits available to SEZ units for 5 years,
3. Exemption from Central seal Tax.
4. Exemption from Service Tax.
5. Single window clearance for Central and State level approval.

Commodity Boards

The functions and activities of commodity boards are similar to that of EPCs. The difference is that the commodity boards look after the export promotion of primary and traditional items of exports while the EPCs look after the export promotions of non traditional items like engineering goods, computers, chemicals, etc while promising export potential.

Commodity boards play a constructive and positive role in the export promotion of primary and traditional commodities such as tea, coffee, rubber, handicrafts, handlooms, coir, etc. these boards offer varied services to government as well as exporters of these commodities. Trade information and guidance is given to exporters. The boards participate in trade fairs and exhibitions and also sponsor trade delegations. Market surveys are conducted for the benefit of exporters and timely advice is given to government on export matters. These services of commodities boards indicate the active interest which the boards take in export promotion and their positive role in promoting exports of traditional commodities. Along with exporters, services are also offered to growers, producers and cultivators of different commodities.

The functional areas of commodity boards are extremely board based. The functions/ activities of commodity boards include market research, publicity, introduction of new methods of cultivation, introduction of new varieties and products for exports and so on.

They also act as a connecting links between India manufacturers/exporters and foreign importers. All these functions are directly and indirectly useful for export promotion of agro based production. The activities of commodity boards are expanding in recent years. There is diversification in functions/activities and services offered by commodity boards. These boards have made substantial contribution in promoting exports of traditional Indian commodities. Their role is certainly unique and praise worthy as export promotion organizations.

Along with Export Promotion Councils, commodity boards have been established by the GOI for many commodities with high export potential. These boards are supplementary to EPCs and function on the same lines. The CBs are for promoting exports of specific commodities particularly the traditional commodities including tea, coffee, rubber and handloom items.

The commodity boards are autonomous bodies. Commodity boards take active interest in introduction of new methods of cultivation of commodities, market research, publicity and assistance to manufacturers and exporters. They act as a connecting link between Indian manufacturers and foreign importers. These boards have open foreign offices. They participate in international trade fairs/exhibitions and also undertake market service and other research activities. Trade delegations are often sent by these boards for promoting exports. Pre-shipment inspection of export items is also arranged by some CBs.

Functions of Commodity Boards

1. Advice to government- the boards offer advice to the government on export matters such a fixing quota for exports and signing trade agreements
2. Registration facility- any exporter concerned with the export of specific commodity can get himself registered with concerned board
3. Provide information- the commodity boards provide trade information, guidance and various other services to the members and help them in their export promotion efforts
4. Trade fairs and exhibitions- the boards participate in trade fairs and exhibitions aboard
5. Sponsor trade delegation- the boards also sponsor trade delegations and conduct market surveys for the benefit of their members
6. To take up various problems, points, suggestions to the States / Central Government and semi- Government Bodies.

7. To take up issues with the Export Promotion Organization - EPCs, Commodity Board, FIEO, ITPO, Various Government Ministries and Departments for Making easy participation in the Fairs and Exhibitions organized in India and Overseas.

8. To make efforts for creation of transparency in the function of the EP Organization-EPCs ,Commodity Board ,FIEO etc.

9. To organize Seminars and Meetings at various places to discuss ways and means to overcome problems and difficulties of the member-exporters / exporting community.

10. To invite Government officials, officials of EP Organizations and Dignitaries at the meetings

11. / Seminars for facilitation and resolving problems relating to exports of the member exporters / exporting community.

12. To publish brochures ,booklets containing useful information for member exporters foreign buyers/ buying agents etc.

13. To distribute the brochures ,booklets ,directories etc. at the time of fair and other occasions for the benefits of member exporters.

14. To set up International Trade Centers and Flatted Factory Complex (Industrial Parks).

15. To unite exporters to take common cause / issues with the concerned Organization Foreign Embassies and Foreign Mission in India and Foreign Trade Offices in India and Indian embassies / High Commissions overseas etc.

Operating Commodity Boards

As the name indicates, every commodity board deals with one specific commodity only. The functions of all boards are rather identical as they are basically concerned with the export promotion of specific commodities. These boards offer different services to exporters, growers, producers and cultivators of various commodities. The commodity boards are statutory in character and operate under the administrative control of the ministry of commerce. There are five statutory Commodity Boards under the Department of Commerce. These Boards are responsible for production, development and export of tea, coffee, rubber, spices and tobacco.

(i) Coffee Board

The Coffee Board is a statutory organisation constituted under Section (4) of the Coffee Act, 1942 and functions under the administrative control of the Ministry of Commerce and Industry, Government of India. The Board comprises 33 Members including the Chairperson, who is the Chief Executive and functions from Bangalore. The remaining 32 Members representing various interests are appointed as per provisions under Section 4(2) of the Coffee Act read with Rule 3 of the Coffee Rules, 1955. The Board is mainly focusing its activities in the areas of research, extension, development, quality upgradation, economic & market intelligence, external & internal promotion and labour welfare. The Board has a Central Coffee Research Institute at Balehonnur (Karnataka) and Regional Coffee Research Stations at Chettalli (Karnataka), Chundale (Kerala), Thandigudi (Tamil Nadu), R.V.Nagar (Andhra Pradesh) and Diphu (Assam), and a bio-technology centre at Mysore, apart from the extension offices located in coffee growing regions of Karnataka, Kerala, Tamil Nadu, Andhra Pradesh, Odissa and North Eastern Region.

(ii) Rubber Board

The Rubber Board is a statutory organisation constituted under Section (4) of the Rubber Act, 1947 and functions under the administrative control of Ministry of Commerce and Industry. The Board is headed by a Chairman appointed by the Central Government and has twenty seven members representing various interests of natural rubber industry. The Board's headquarters is located at Kottayam in Kerala. The Board is responsible for the development of the rubber industry in the country by way of assisting and encouraging research, development, extension and training activities related to rubber. It also maintains statistical data of rubber, takes steps to promote marketing of rubber and undertake labour welfare activities. The activities of the Board are exercised through nine departments viz. Rubber Production, Research, Processing & Product Development, Training, License & Excise Duty, Statistics and Planning, Market Promotion, Finance & Accounts and Administration. The Board has five Zonal Offices and 43 Regional Offices. It has a Central Rubber Research Institute in Kottayam and 10 regional research stations located in various rubber growing states of the country. It also has a Rubber Training Institute located at Kottayam.

(iii) Tea Board

Tea Board was set up as a statutory body on 1st April, 1954 as per Section (4) of the Tea Act, 1953. As an apex body, it looks after the overall development of the tea industry. The Board is headed by a Chairman and consists of 30 Members appointed by the Government of India representing various interests pertaining to tea industry. The Board's Head Office is situated in Kolkata and there are two Zonal offices-one each in North Eastern Region at Jorhat in Assam and in Southern Region at Coonoor in Tamil Nadu. Besides, there are fifteen regional offices spread over in all the major tea growing states and four metros. For the purpose of tea promotion, three overseas offices are located at London, Moscow and Dubai. During the year under report a separate directorate has been established to look after the developmental needs of the small tea sector in the country. Several Sub regional offices have been opened in all the important areas of small growers concentration to maintain a closer interface with the growers. The functions and responsibilities of Tea Board include increasing production and productivity, improving the quality of tea, market promotion, welfare measures for plantation workers and supporting Research and Development. Collection, collation and dissemination of statistical information to all stake holders are yet another important function of the Board. Being the regulatory body, the Board exerts control over the producers, manufacturers, exporters, tea brokers, auction organisers and warehouse keepers through various control orders notified under Tea Act.

(iv) Tobacco Board

The Tobacco Board was constituted as a statutory body on 1st January, 1976 under Section (4) of the Tobacco Board Act, 1975. The Board is headed by a Chairman with its headquarters at Guntur, Andhra Pradesh and is responsible for the development of the tobacco industry. While the primary function of the Board is export promotion of all varieties of tobacco and its allied products, its functions extend to production, distribution

(v) Spices Board

The Spices Board was constituted as a statutory body on 26th February, 1987 under Section (3) of the Spices Board Act, 1986. The Board is headed by a Chairman appointed by Central Government and consists of 32 members. The Board's Head Office is at Kochi with Regional/ Zonal/ Field offices throughout India. It is responsible for the development of cardamom industry and export promotion of the 52 spices listed in the Schedule of the Spices Board Act, 1986. The primary functions of the Board include production development of small and large cardamom, development and promotion of export of spices. The Board is also implementing programmes for development of spices in North Eastern region, post- harvest improvement of spices and organic spices in the country. The activities of the Board include issue of certificate of registration as exporter of spices; undertaking programmes and projects for promotion of export of spices like setting up of spices parks, support of infrastructure improvement in spices processing, assisting and encouraging studies and research on medicinal properties of spices, development of new products, improvement of processing, grading and packaging of spices; and controlling & upgrading quality for export (including setting up of regional quality evaluation labs and training centres). With regard to cardamom, the Board's licenced auctioneers and dealers facilitate the domestic marketing through e-auctions. The research activities on cardamom are also done by the Board through its Indian Cardamom Research Institute.

The Marine Products Export Development Authority

The Marine Products Export Development Authority (MPEDA) was constituted in 1972 under the Marine Products Export Development Authority Act 1972(No.13 of 1972). The role envisaged for the MPEDA under the statue is comprehensive – covering fisheries of all kinds, increasing exports, specifying standards, processing, marketing, extension and training in various aspects of the industry. MPEDA functions under the Ministry of Commerce, Government of India and acts as a coordinating agency with different Central and State Government establishments engaged in fishery production and allied activities.

Standing Committees of MPEDA

1. Executive Committee
2. Technical Committee
3. Export Promotion Committee

The plan schemes of the Authority are implemented under seven major heads:

1. Market Promotion
2. Capture Fisheries
3. Culture Fisheries
4. Processing infrastructure & value addition
5. Quality control
6. Research and development
7. Viability gap funding

Work Programme of MPEDA

1. Registration of infrastructure facilities for seafood Export trade
2. Collection and dissemination of trade information
3. Projection of Indian marine products in overseas markets by participation in overseas fairs and organising international seafood fairs in India.
4. Implementation of development measures
5. Promotion of aquaculture for production of shrimp and prawn for export.
6. Promotion of value added Sea foods.
7. Promotion of Tuna fishery.
8. Implementation of organic farming.
9. Conservation management.

Agricultural and processed Food Products Export Development Authority

The Agricultural and Processed Food Products Export Development Authority (APEDA) was established by the Government of India under the Agricultural and Processed Food Products Export Development Authority Act passed by the Parliament in December, 1985. The Authority, with its headquarters at New Delhi, is headed by a Chairperson. APEDA has been serving the agri-export community since its inception. To reach out to the exporters in different parts of the country, in addition to 5 Regional Offices, APEDA has set up 13 Virtual Offices at Thiruvananthapuram (Kerala), Bhubaneshwar (Orissa), Srinagar (J&K), Chandigarh, Imphal (Manipur), Agartala (Tripura), Kohima (Nagaland), Chennai (Tamil Nadu), Raipur (Chhatisgarh), Ahmedabad (Gujarat), Bhopal (Madhya Pradesh), Lucknow (Uttar Pradesh) and Panaji (Goa). APEDA has been entrusted with the responsibility of export promotion and development of 14 agricultural and processed food product groups listed in the Schedule to the APEDA Act. In addition to this, APEDA has been entrusted with the responsibility to monitor the import of sugar as well.

APEDA has been actively engaged in the development of markets besides upgradation of infrastructure and quality to promote the export of agro products. In its endeavour to promote agro exports, APEDA provides financial assistance to the registered exporters under its Schemes for Market Development, Infrastructure Development, Quality Development and Transport Assistance.

The mandate of the Department of Commerce is regulation, development and promotion of India's international trade and commerce through formulation of appropriate international trade & commercial policy and implementation of the various provisions thereof. The basic role of the Department is to facilitate the creation of an enabling environment and infrastructure for accelerated growth of international trade. The Department formulates, implements and monitors the Foreign Trade Policy (FTP) which provides the basic framework of policy and strategy to be followed for promoting exports and trade. The Trade Policy is periodically reviewed to incorporate changes necessary to take care of emerging economic scenarios both in the domestic and international economy. Besides, the Department is also entrusted with responsibilities relating to multilateral and bilateral commercial relations, Special Economic Zones, state trading, export promotion and trade facilitation, and development and regulation of certain export oriented industries and commodities. The Department is headed by a Secretary who is assisted by an Additional Secretary & Financial Advisor, four Additional Secretary and eleven Joint Secretaries & Joint Secretary level officers and a number of other senior officers.

The Indian Institute of Foreign Trade

The Indian Institute of Foreign Trade (IIFT) was set up in 1963 by the Government of India as an autonomous organisation to help professionalise the country's foreign trade management and increase exports by developing human resources; generating, analysing and disseminating data; and conducting research. The Institute is acting as a catalyst for new ideas, concepts and skills for the internationalisation of the Indian economy. The institute is acting as a primary provider of training and research-based consultancy in the areas of international business, for the corporate sector, Government and the student community, at large. It is an institution with proven capability to continuously upgrade its knowledge base with a view to meet the requirements of the Government, trade and industry through both sponsored and non-sponsored research and consultancy assignments.

Functions of Indian Institute of Foreign Trade

a) Training

The IIFT has been recognised as a centre excellence for imparting training and education in international, business. Its specialisation in international business and a global outlook makes it unique among management schools in the country. It offers an inspiring learning environment, which transforms the bright young students into talented creative professionals.

b) Collects and Supplies Information

It conducts market studies and surveys in the overseas markets. It tries to find out demand for Indian products in overseas market. It supplies this information to the exporters. The exporters can use such information while making their export marketing decisions.

c) Organises Seminars and Workshops

The institute organises seminars and workshops in a number of export marketing areas, such as export pricing, export promotion, etc. Exporters can take advantage of such workshops and seminars by taking active part them.

d) Trade Delegations

It sends delegates abroad to study overseas markets and also to interact with overseas importers. At the same time, it invites delegates from abroad, who cal study Indian market conditions and can also interact with Indian exporters.

e) Publications

A large part of the llFT's research work is published in the form of study reports, monographs, status papers, etc. for wider dissemination among the business community, government departments and academic fields. The institute publishers

f) Research and Consultancy

Indian Institute of Foreign Trade has so far brought out year 570 research studies and surveys. It also acts as a consulting house for solving the problems of the exporters and importers. It analyses the international business environment and develops appropriate corporate strategies for the overseas markets.

g) Management Development Programmes

Combining a unique blend of research and consultancy, the institute has been a pacesetter in addressing to the needs of business executives by continuously aligning the focus of its Management Development Programmes with the changing realities. As a result, its intensive short duration programmes have received the most enthusiastic response.

Indian Trade Promotion Organisation (ITPO)

Indian Trade Promotion Organisation was set up by the Ministry of Commerce, Government of India, on 1st January 1992 with its headquarters at New Delhi after the merger of Trade Development Authority and Trade Fair Authority of India. As a premier trade promotion agency of the Government of India the ITPO provides a broad spectrum of services to trade and industry so as to catalyse the growth of bilateral trade, particularity India's exports and technological up gradation and modernisation of industry segments.

India Trade Promotion Organisation, the nodal trade promotion agency of the Government of India, has been charting a multi-dimensional course in conformity with its mandated role. Since its inception and prior to that in its erstwhile incarnations of Trade Fair Authority of India and Trade Development Authority, ITPO has, for well over three decades, played a multi-faceted role in bringing out the strengths of the Indian economy through a focused seven band spectrum of activity.

Functions of Indian Trade Promotion Organisation (ITPO)

a) Organizes Various Trade Fairs and Exhibitions

It organizes various trade fairs and exhibitions at its exhibition complex in Pragati Maidan, New Delhi and other centres in India. It also extends the use of Pragati Maidan for holding of trade fairs and exhibitions by other fair organisers both from India and abroad.

b) Involves the State Governments

It enlists the involvement and support of the State Governments for the promotion of India's foreign trade. It promotes establishment of facilities and infrastructure for holding trade fairs in state capitals or other suitable locations in India, in consultation with the State Governments concerned.

c) Assists in Technological Up gradation and Product Development

It provides assistance to Indian companies in locating suitable foreign collaborators for transfer of technology, joint ventures, marketing tie-ups and investment promotion. It also assists Indian companies in product development and helps them to adapt to meet buyer's requirements.

d) Helps in Establishing Overseas Contacts

It helps in establishing durable contacts between Indian suppliers and overseas buyers. It organises buyer-seller meets with a view to bring buyers and sellers together. It also invites overseas buyers and organises their meetings with Indian suppliers.

e) Other Services

1. To identify and nurture specific export products with long- range growth prospects.
2. To conduct in-house and need-based research on trade and export promotion.
3. Export Import Procedures & Documentation
4. To participate in overseas trade fairs and exhibitions.
5. To organise seminars, conferences and workshops.
6. To encourage and involve small and medium scale units in export promotion efforts.
7. Timely and efficient services to overseas buyers
8. Establishing durable contacts between Indian suppliers and overseas buyers
9. Organising Buyer-Seller Meets
10. Arranging product displays for visiting overseas buyers
11. Trade information services through electronic accessibility
12. Conducting in-house and need-based research on trade and export promotion

National Centre for Trade Information

National Centre for Trade Information (NCTI) was incorporated on 31st March, 1995 as a Company under. The Company started functioning from 1996 as a nonprofit making company. It offers unparalleled advantages in terms of business efficiency and cutting down costs. By saving valuable time needed for searching for information on a wide range of business related topics, the institute allows its members to utilise their time more efficiently. It accesses databases prepared by various private and Government companies for their clients and caters to a large number of users in India and Abroad. Thus, NCTI provides convenient one stop for all business information needs.

It has a Board of Directors for administration of its affairs, which includes representatives from Ministry of Commerce & Industry, National Informatics Centre, Indian Institute of Foreign trade, and Directorate General of Commercial Intelligence & Statistics (DGCI&S). Other representatives are from India Trade Promotion Organisation (ITPO) and other Export Promotion Councils. NCTI provides value added trade information for the benefit of the international trading community. National Centre for Trade Information is a joint venture of India Trade Promotion Organisation and National Informatics Centre under the aegis of Ministry of Commerce, Government of India..

Functions NCTI

1. Setting up and Management of a Computerized Trade Information Centre at Karnataka.
2. Development of Module for Online Evaluation and monitoring system.
3. Handicrafts study for Development Commissioner of Handicrafts.
4. Development and maintenance of websites for India Trade Promotion Organisation.
5. Indian Institute Packaging (IIP)

Indian Institute of Packaging was set up as a national institute jointly by the Ministry of Commerce, Government of India, and the Indian Packaging industry and allied interests in 1966, with its head quarters and principal laboratories at Mumbai and regional laboratories at Kolkata, Delhi and Chennai. It is a training-cum-research institute pertaining to packaging and testing. Over the years, it has built up a very strong and capable expertise in various fields of packaging sciences and technologies. It has excellent infrastructural facilities, which cater to the various needs of the package manufacturing and package user industries, both with regard to the domestic distribution and export market Requirements.

Functions of Indian Institute of Packaging

a) Training Programmes

It organises a number of training programmes pertaining to packaging and also provides suggestions in regard to packaging.

b) Testing Facilities

It also undertakes testing of packaging materials and packages to ensure export quality.

c) UN Certification

All dangerous goods packages need a UN certification mark before they can be dispatched. IIP is the only authorised body in India to give this certification.

d) Environmental Cell

The institute has an environment cell, which guides exporters as to what type of material can be used or incorporated in the packaging of their products so as to reduce environmental threats.

e) Research and Development

It undertakes research and development programmes for creating and improving overall infrastructure facilities for achieving packaging improvements as to prevent losses during transportation.

f) Collection and Dissemination of Information

It collects information on various packing and packaging strategies and disseminates them to the exporter for their benefits. Up-to-date information on packaging developments can be availed its official website.

g) International Recognition

The institute is closely linked international organisations. It is recognised by the Unit® Nations Industrial Development Organisation (UNIDOJ International Trading Centre (ITC) for consultancy and training

h) International Membership

It is a member of the Asian Packaging Federation (APF); the Institute of Packaging Professionals (IOPPA), USA; the Institute of Packaging OOP) UK; Technical Association for Pulp and Paper Industry (TAPPI) and the World Packaging Organisation (WPO).

Indian Council of Arbitration (ICA)

International Court of Arbitration (ICA) was set up in accordance to the recommendations of the Committee on Commercial Arbitration constituted by the Ministry of Commerce, Government of India. It was set up on 15th April 1965 as an autonomous non-profit organisation registered under the societies Registration Act, 19670. The main objective of the Council is to promote the use of commercial arbitration, particularly in the course of India's export trade. ICA is member of the Federation of International Commercial Arbitral Institution and has mutual co-operation agreements with the International Court of Arbitration, the

London Court of Arbitration and apex arbitration bodies in Thailand, Republic of Korea, Yugoslavia, Bulgaria, Romania, Malaysia, Australia, USA, Denmark, Mauritius, Russia, Germany, Egypt, Switzerland, Japan, Philippines, Sri Lanka, South Africa and more.

Functions of Indian Council of Arbitration

1. Arbitration Facilities

The council provides arbitration facilities for all types of domestic and international commercial disputes.

2. Conciliation of International Trade Complaints

It uses its network of offices for conciliation of international trade complaints received from Indian and foreign parties, for non-performance of contracts or non-compliance with arbitration awards.

3. Arbitration Meetings

It organises arbitration meetings, conferences, training programmes, etc., for company executives, businessmen, lawyers, arbitrators, etc., from time to time in different parts of the country.

4. Research and Publications

It conducts research and publishes informative literature on different aspects of commercial arbitration, including a quarterly Arbitration Journal.

5. Dissemination of Information

It provides information and advice to interested parties regarding the drafting of trade contracts, arbitration laws and facilities and dispute settlement procedures in India and in other parts of the world.

6. Updating Developments

It keeps abreast of the latest developments, in the field of international commercial arbitration and maintains co-operative links with national and international arbitration bodies throughout the world.

Federation of Indian Export Organisation (FIEO)

Federation of India Export Organisations (FIEO) is an apex body of various export promotion organisations. It was set up in October 1965. It represents the Indian entrepreneurs' spirit of enterprise in the global market. It has kept pace with the country's evolving economic and trade policies and has provided the content, direction and thrust to India's expanding international trade. As the apex body of all Indian export promotion organisations, FIEO works as a partner of the Government of India to promote Indian exports.

Functions of Federation of Indian Export Organisation

a) International Linkage

It has forged strong links with counterpart organisations in several countries as well as international agencies to enable direct communications and interaction between India world businessmen. It is registered with UNCTAD as a national non-government organisation, and has direct access to information and data originating from UN bodies and world agencies like IMF, ADB, World Bank and others.

b) Dissemination of Information

It has bilateral arrangements for exchange of information as well as for liaison with several overseas chambers commerce and trade and industry associations.

c) Liaison with the Government

It sends representations on policy matters to Central Governments. It helps in establishing contacts between the government and commercial bodies both in India and overseas.

d) Market Development Assistance (MDA)

FIEO reimburses certain percentage of the expenditure incurred by the recognised exporters, such as all types of export houses sales-cum-study tours, participation in exhibitions and abroad, advertisements in foreign media, etc.

e) Market Research and Development Department

The Market Research and Development department offers the following services to the exporters' community.

1. Arranging meetings with diplomats, incoming delegation and buying missions.
2. Inviting delegations
3. Organising trade fairs and exhibitions in India and abroad
4. Opening foreign offices and warehouses
5. Organising seminars for promotion of international trade
6. Opening new FIEO offices abroad

f) Publicity Department

Bringing out various special supplements in Indian and overseas dailies in order to project the selected finished products in India and abroad. Creating and telecasting episodes in NEPC channel to promote India's prominent brands in various countries covered by the channel. It has published Directory of Foreign Buyers and Dictionary of Indian Exporters. It publishes a fortnightly magazine, 'FIEO News', to cover developments in the field of international trade concerning India.

Board of Trade

The Board of Trade has been revamped and given a clear and dynamic role in advising government on relevant issues connected with Foreign Trade Policy. It has been proposed in the Foreign Trade Policy 2004-09 to have a process of continuous interaction between the Board of Trade and Government in order to achieve the desired objective of boosting India's exports.

Functions of Board of Trade

The Board of Trade Renders the following Functions

- Advise the Government on Policy measures for preparation
- Implementation of both short and long term plans for increasing exports in the light of emerging national and international economic scenarios;
- Review export performance of various sectors, identify constraints and suggest industry specific measures to optimize export earnings;
- Examine the existing institutional framework for imports & exports and suggest practical measures for further streamlining to achieve the desired objectives;
- Review the policy instruments and procedures for imports & exports and suggest steps to rationalize and channelise such schemes for optimum use;
- Examine issues which are considered relevant for promotion of India's foreign trade, and to strengthen the international competitiveness of Indian goods and services;
- Conducting studies for furtherance of the above objectives.

Export Inspection Council

Export Inspection Council of India was set up by the Government of India under Section 3 of the Export (Quality Control and Inspection) Act, 1963, to provide for the sound development of export trade through quality control and pre-shipment inspection. The Council is an apex body for controlling the activities of quality control and pre- shipment inspection of all the commodities meant for export.

Methods of Pre-shipment Inspection and Quality Control

Export Inspection Council has three recognised systems of inspection for the purpose of pre-shipment inspection.

a) Consignment-wise Inspection

Under the Consignment wise Inspection each export consignment is inspected a tested by the recognised inspection agencies. Samples drawn on the basis of statistical sampling plans are inspected and test for verifying the conformity of products to the prescribe standards. Tests are carried out in the field and/or in to recognised inspection agencies or laboratories.

A certificate is issued for the consignment if it is found export worthy after inspection. Depending on the nature of consignment, the certificate of inspection has varying validity periods on the expiry of which the consignments are re-inspected for the purpose of revalidation of the certificate. No consignment of any notified commodity can be exported unless it is accompanied by a certificate issued by a recognised; inspection agency or it carries a recognised mark, as may applicable to it.

b) In-Process Quality Control

In-Process Quality Control system lays emphasis on the responsibility of manufacturer processors in ensuring consistency in quality during all stages of production by adopting quality control drills and exercising control on raw materials and bought-out components manufacturing process, packing and final testing. Manufacturing and processing units, adjudged as having adequate levels of quality control in all these areas are eligible to get certificate of export worthiness without further verification.

c) Self-Certification

Under this system, stringent requirements have been prescribed for four, new elements namely design and development, quality audit, after sales and service, housekeeping and maintenance. Manufacturing and processing units qualifying under this system are notified by the Government as Agencies to issue certificates of export worthiness for their own export consignments. This facility is offered initially for one year and their performance is subject to review. This facility is introduced in engineering scheme only to begin with and depending upon the efficiency of the scheme, it, may be introduced for other schemes.

d) Food Safety Management System Based Certification

In view of growing concern all over the world regarding health and safety parameters of food items being imported, international standards on Food Safety Management Systems have been developed. Based on such standards, which are being prescribed by several of India's trading partners of European Union, EIC has introduced certification of product quality integrated with the systems approach. Currently, fish and fishery products, egg products and milk products are being certified under the above system.

Functions of Export Inspection Council

a) Advisory to the Government

The EIC advises the Indian Government on matters relating to pre-shipment inspection and quality control measures for export items by defining the technical specifications for various products; Providing testing and survey facilities; and Working out appropriate procedures for quality control.

b) Export Inspection Agencies

In addition to the main offices of EIAs at Bombay, Kolkata, Cochin, Delhi and Chennai, these i' agencies have a network of 62 sub-offices located at important manufacturing and processing centres, ports and export points. These agencies have well equipped laboratories at all important centres for inspection and testing of the products offered by exporters or manufacturers for inspection.

c) Pilot Test House

A Pilot Test House has been set up in Mumbai with necessary infrastructural facilities of testing the products to meet the requirements of the international standards. The Test House has three major sectional laboratories namely Chemical laboratory, Electric laboratory and Mechanical laboratory

d) Training Facilities

In order to achieve the overall objective^ the export development through quality control and inspection the Export Inspection Council has set up a full-fledged training centre at Chennai where training is imparted to the inspecting officers. The inspecting officers are given training on the methodology and techniques of quality assurance including latest techniques in standardisation, inspection and quality control prevalent in other countries.

e) Voluntary Inspection

In addition to carrying out compulsory quality control and pre-shipment inspection of commodities notified by the government under the Export (Quality Control) Inspection Act, 1963, the EIC undertakes voluntary pre-shipment inspection at the specific requests received from foreign buyers or Indian exporters. Such inspection is carried out on the basis of the specifications mutually agreed between the buyer and the seller.

f) GSP Certification

An important function of the Export Inspection Council is to issue certificate of origin under the Generalised System of Preference (GSP) required for specified products exported to preference, giving countries of Europe, America, Japan, etc.

Export Credit and Guarantee Corporation

The ECGC a Government of India undertaking has been established for minimizing the risk element in export business and to facilitate the flow of finance from the banks to exporters. In addition to the normal risk policies, the corporation assists the exporters through special schemes such as packing credit guarantee, post shipment credit guarantee and export production finance guarantee. To suit varying needs of exporters, the corporation provides different types of cover which may be divided into the following three broad groups: Standard polices Financial guarantees Special policies Under its policies intended to protect the exporters against overseas credit risks, ECGC bears the main risks and pays the exporter 90% of his loss on account of commercial risks and Political risks.

Export-Import Bank

The EXIM Bank was established on January 1, 1982 for the purpose of financing, facilitating and promoting foreign trade of India. It extends finance to exporters of capital and manufactured goods, exporters of software's and consultancy services and overseas joint ventures and construction projects abroad. The bank is the principal financial institution in India for coordinating the work of institutions engaged in financing export and import trade. The EXIM bank concentrates mainly on medium and long term credit for export of goods and services on deferred payment terms.

EXPORT INCENTIVES AND FACILITIES

Introduction

Export Incentives are motivating factors provided by Indian Government to boost exports and help to exporters in competitive foreign markets. These incentives and facilities relate to exports performance, promotion of exports, fiscal incentives, schemes aimed at facilitation of imports for exports and various subsidies. Some export benefits are classified in form of Duty Drawback, Tax Concession MDA, EPCG, DFIA, VKGUY, SFIS, SHIS, FPS, MLFPS & Focus Market Product Schemes.

Duty Drawbacks

Drawback means the refund of duty of customs and duty of central excise that are chargeable on imported and indigenous materials used in the manufacture of exported goods. A refund that can be obtained when an import fee has already been paid for a good, but the good is then subsequently exported. In order to obtain a duty drawback, a business does not have to have paid the import duty, nor do they have had to perform the product's exportation, they only need to be assigned the drawback from those to whom it would typically be due. The term drawback is applied to a certain amount of duties of Customs and Central Excise, sometimes the whole, sometimes only a part remitted or paid by Government on the exportation of the commodities on which they were levied. To entitle goods to drawback, they must be exported to a foreign port, the object of the relief afforded by the drawback being to enable the goods to be disposed of in the foreign market as if they had never been taxed at all. Goods eligible for drawback applies to

- Export goods imported into India as such;
- Export goods imported into India after having been taken for use
- Export goods manufactured / produced out of imported material
- Export goods manufactured / produced out of indigenous material
- Export goods manufactured /produced out of imported or and indigenous materials.

Types of Duty Drawback

The Duty Drawback is of Two Types

i. All Industry Rate (AIR) and
ii. Brand Rate.

i.   The All Industry Rate (AIR) is essentially an average rate based on the average quantity and value of inputs and duties (both Excise & Customs) borne by them and Service Tax suffered by a particular export product. The All Industry Rates are notified by the Government in the form of a Drawback Schedule every year. The All Industry Rate (AIR) of Duty Drawback is generally fixed as a percentage of FOB prices of export product. Caps have been imposed in respect of many export products in order to obviate the possibility of misuse by unscrupulous exporters through over invoicing of the export value. The All Industry Rate (AIR) of Duty Drawback are notified for a large number of export products every year by the Government after an assessment of average incidence of Customs, Central Excise duties and Service Tax suffered by the export products.

ii.   The Brand Rate of Duty Drawback is allowed in cases where the export product does not have any AIR of Duty Drawback or the same neutralizes less than 4/5th of the duties paid on materials used in the manufacture of export goods. This work is handled by the jurisdictional Commissioners of Customs & Central Excise. Exporters who wish to avail of the Brand Rate of Duty Drawback need to apply for fixation of the rate for their export goods to the jurisdictional Central Excise Commissionerate. Under this scheme, the exporters are compensated by paying the amount of Customs, Central Excise duties and Service Tax incidence actually incurred by the export product. For this purpose, the exporter has to produce documents/proof about the actual quantity of inputs / services utilized in the manufacture of export product along with evidence of payment of duties thereon.

Imported Goods re-exported-Drawback

Customs Duty paid at the time of import of the goods, can be claimed as Duty Drawback at the time of export of such goods. For this purpose, the identity of export goods is cross verified with the particulars furnished at the time of import of such goods.

The elements necessary to claim this drawback are;

1.   The goods on which drawback is claimed must have been previously imported;

2.   Import duty must have been paid on these goods when they were imported;

3.   The goods should be entered for export within two years from the date of payment of duty

4.   The goods are identified as the goods imported.

5.   The goods must be capable of being identified as imported goods.

6. The goods must actually be re-exported to any place outside India.

7. The market price of such goods must not be less than the amount of drawback claimed.

AIR Duty Drawback 2013

The Union ministry of finance has notified an increase in the All Industry Rates (AIR) of duty drawback and higher value caps for many items. The major beneficiaries are exporters of textiles, vehicles and automobile components. When the All Industry Rate (AIR) for 2013-14 were notified on September 14, 2013, exporters had expressed disappointment over the reduction in rates for many items, as well as the value caps that limited the drawback amount payable. Exporters of electronics goods had expressed concern on the sharp decline in drawback rates on their items. Exporters of engineering goods had reacted strongly and said the reduction would negate the positive impact of rupee depreciation. The exporters of textiles represented that averaging the duty incidence of many items at the four-digit levels resulted in anomalies.

Duty Free Replenishment Certificate

Duty Free Replenishment Certificate is issued to a merchant-exporter or manufacturer-exporter for the import of inputs used in the manufacture of goods without payment of Basic Customs Duty, Surcharge and Special Additional Duty. However, such inputs shall be subject to the payment of Additional Customs Duty equal to the Excise Duty at the time of import. Duty Free Replenishment Certificate shall be issued only in respect of export products as notified by DGFT. The export products, which are eligible for modified VAT, shall be eligible for CENVAT credit however, non excisable, non dutiable or non centrally vatable products, shall be eligible for drawback at the time of exports in lieu of additional customs duty to be paid at the time of imports under the scheme. The exporter shall be entitled for drawback benefits in respect of any of the duty paid materials, whether imported or indigenous, used in the export product as per the drawback rate fixed by Directorate of Drawback. The drawback shall however be restricted to the duty paid materials not covered under Standard Input and Output Norms (SION)

Duty Free Import Authorization Scheme

DFIA is scheme is in existence from 1st May, 2006. A Duty Free Import Authorisation is issued to allow duty free import of inputs which are used in the manufacture of the export product (making normal allowance for wastage) and fuel, energy, catalyst etc. which

Special Import Licence

It is a permit that allows an importer to bring in a specified quantity of certain goods during a specified period (usually one year). Import licenses are employed as means of restricting outflow of foreign currency to improve a country's balance of payments position; to control entry of dangerous items such as explosives, firearms, and certain substances; or to protect the domestic industry from foreign competition. An import license is a document issued by a national government authorizing the importation of certain goods into its territory. Import licenses are considered to be non-tariff barriers to trade when used as a way to discriminate against another country's goods in order to protect a domestic industry from foreign competition.

Served From India Scheme

Government of India has introduced "Served from India Scheme" to facilitate exporter of various type of services. The objective of this scheme is to accelerate growth in export of services so as to create a powerful and unique 'Served From India' brand, instantly recognized and respected world over.

Under this scheme, Service Providers of more than 100 services like Professional Services, Computer Related services, Hotels, Restaurants, Educational Services, Research and Development services, Communication Services, Construction and Related Engineering Services, Distribution Service, Environmental related Services, Tourism and Transport related Services, Health Related Social Service, Recreational, Cultural and Sporting Services. The government's decision to allow companies to spread the benefit of goods imported under the 'Served from India' scheme among group companies is expected to help diversified business groups and software companies. The Foreign Trade Policy announced today allows companies to extend the benefits from the scheme to group companies so as to enable service providers to upgrade infrastructure in associate firms.

Vishesh Krishi and Gram Udyog Yojana Scheme

The objective of VKGUY is to promote exports of:
- Agricultural Produce and their value added products;
- Minor Forest Produce and their value added variants;
- Gram Udyog Products;
- Forest Based Products; and
- Other Products, as notified from time to time.

Duty Credit Scrip benefits are granted with an aim to compensate high transport costs, and to offset other disadvantages.

Status Holder Incentive Scrip

With an objective to promote investment in up gradation of technology of some specified sectors, Status Holders exporting products of these sectors shall be entitled to incentive scrip

@1% of FOB value of exports in the form of duty credit. The Status Holders Incentive Scrip shall be with Actual User Condition and shall be used for imports of capital goods related to the sector.

Agri-Infrastructure Scrip

For exports made during a particular year, all Status Holders exporting products covered under ITC HS Chapters 1 to 24, shall be incentivized with duty credit scrip equal to 10% of FOB value of agricultural exports (including VKGUY benefits entitled under Policy Para 3.13.2) provided that the total benefits for all status holders put together does not exceed Rs 100 Cr (i.e. Rs 50 Cr for each half year). Zonal Office, CLA, New Delhi is the licensing office for grant of this benefit to all status holders of the country.

Focus Product Scheme

The objective is to incentives export of such products which have high export intensity / employment potential, so as to offset infrastructure inefficiencies and other associated costs involved in marketing of these products. Exports of notified products (as in Appendix 37D of HBPv1) to all countries (including SEZ units) shall be entitled for Duty Credit scrip equivalent to 2% of FOB value of exports. However, Special Focus Product(s) /sector(s), covered under Table 2 and Table 5 of Appendix 37D, shall be granted Duty Credit Scrip equivalent to 5% of FOB value of exports. Further, Focus Product(s) / sector(s) that are notified under Table 7 of Appendix 37D shall be granted Additional Duty Credit Scrip equivalent to 2% of FOB value of export.

Market Linked Focus Product Scheme

Export of Products/Sectors of high export intensity / employment potential (which are not covered under present FPS List) would be incentivized at 2% of FOB value of exports (in free foreign exchange) under FPS when exported to the Linked Markets (countries), which are not covered in the present FMS list.

Focus Market Scheme

Objective of this scheme is to offset high freight cost and other externalities to select international markets with a view to enhance India's export competitiveness in these countries. Exporters of all products to notified countries (as in Appendix 37C of HBPv1) shall be entitled for Duty Credit Scrip equivalent to 3% of FOB value of exports (in free foreign exchange) for exports made from 27.8.2009 onwards

Services Exports from India Scheme

Served from India Scheme (SFIS) has been replaced with Service Exports from India Scheme (SEIS). SEIS shall apply to 'Service Providers located in India' instead of 'Indian Service

Providers'. Thus SEIS provides for rewards to all Service providers of notified services, who are providing services from India, regardless of the constitution or profile of the service provider. The rate of reward under SEIS would be based on net foreign exchange earned. The reward issued as duty credit scrip, would no longer be with actual user condition and will no longer be restricted to usage for specified types of goods but be freely transferable and usable for all types of goods and service tax debits on procurement of services / goods. Debits would be eligible for CENVAT credit or drawback.

Merchandise Exports from India Scheme

Earlier there were 5 different schemes (Focus Product Scheme, Market Linked Focus Product cheme, Focus Market Scheme, Agri. Infrastructure Incentive Scrip, VKGUY) for rewarding erchandise exports with different kinds of duty scrips with varying conditions (sector specific or actual user only) attached to their use. Now all these schemes have been merged into a single scheme, namely Merchandise Export from India Scheme (MEIS) and there would be no conditionality attached to the scrips issued under the scheme. Rewards for export of notified goods to notified markets under 'Merchandise Exports from India Scheme (MEIS) shall be payable as percentage of realized FOB value (in free foreign exchange). The debits towards basic customs duty in the transferable reward duty credit scrips would also be allowed adjustment as duty drawback. At present, only the additional duty of customs / excise duty / service tax is allowed adjustment as CENVAT credit or drawback, as per Department of Revenue rules.

Facilities to Exporters

1) Marketing Development Assistance

Export Promotion continues to be a major thrust area for the Government. In view of the prevailing macro economic situation with emphasis on exports and to facilitate various measures being undertaken to stimulate and diversify the country's export trade, Marketing Development Assistance (MDA) Scheme is under operation through the Department of Commerce to support the under mentioned activities:

i.   Assist exporters for export promotion activities abroad

ii.   Assist Export Promotion Councils (EPCs) to undertake export promotion activities for their product(s) and commodities;

iii.   Assist approved organization/trade bodies in undertaking exclusive nonrecurring innovative activities connected with export promotion efforts for their members;

iv.   Assist Focus export promotion programmes in specific regions; and

v.   Residual essential activities connected with marketing promotion efforts abroad.

Under Reverse trade visits for prominent delegates and Buyers (one person from each organization) for participation in buyer cum Seller meets, exhibitions etc. in India from the Focus Area Regions, exhibitions etc. in India, the foreign delegates/ buyer/journalists would be assisted in meeting their return air travel expenses in economy excursion class up to the entry point in India.

2) Air Freight Subsidies on Export of Horticulture and Floriculture Products

In order to make exports of horticulture (i.e. specified fresh fruits and specified fresh vegetables) and floriculture products competitive in the world market, the Government grants air freight subsidy on selected fruits and floriculture items. Department of Agriculture and Cooperation under the Ministry of Agriculture is the nodal organization responsible for development of the floriculture sector. It is responsible for formulation and implementation of national policies and programmes aimed at achieving rapid agricultural growth through optimum utilization of land, water, soil and plant resources of the country. Production of cut flowers for exports is also a thrust area for support. The Agricultural and Processed Food Products Export Development Authority (APEDA), the nodal organization for promotion of agri exports including flowers, has introduced several schemes for promoting floriculture exports from the country. These relate to development of infrastructure, packaging, market development, subsidy on airfreight for export of cut flowers and tissue-cultured plants, database up-gradation etc. The 100% Export Oriented Units are also given benefits like duty free imports of capital goods. Import duties have also been reduced on cut flowers, flower seeds, tissue-cultured plants, etc. Setting up of walk in type cold storage has been allowed at the International airports for storage of export produce.

Several schemes have been initiated by the Government for promotion and development of the floriculture sector including "Integrated Development of Commercial Floriculture" which aims at improvement in production and productivity of traditional as well as cut flowers through availability of quality planting material, production of off season and quality flowers through protected cultivation, improvement in post harvest handling of flowers and training persons for a scientific floriculture. Many state governments have set up separate departments for promotion of floriculture in their respective states.

3) Assistance for Product Promotion and Packaging Development Schemes of the Spices Board

There are three components under the programme of "Trade Promotion" viz.

1. Sending Business Samples Abroad
2. Printing Promotional Literatures/Brochures

3.   Packaging Development and Bar Coding Registration are supported for promoting spices and spice products. Providing assistance for these components are essential for developing export business, securing orders, better presentation of capabilities to the buyers and to promote modern/scientific packaging for retail market by which the country may build up better image, increased shelf life for the products and higher value realization.

(1) Sending Business Samples Abroad

For finalizing the transactions on the basis of samples and to provide more clarity in dealings and also to eliminate the possibility for trade disputes on quality aspects, the Board is providing assistance for sending business samples of spices and spice products abroad. Under this component, the Board supports the exporters by reimbursing the cost of courier charges.

(2) Printing Promotional Literatures/Brochures

Under this component, the Board offers financial assistance to qualified exporters of spices/spice products to bring out good promotional literatures/ brochures/video films/CDs and other electronic modes.

(3) Packaging Development and Bar Coding for Promoting Spices and Spice Products

For improving the existing packaging and develop modern packaging for increased shelf life, reduce storage space, establishing traceability and better presentation of Indian spices in markets abroad, financial assistance is provided by the Board.

4) Subsidy Schemes of APEDA for Agricultural, Horticultural and Meat Products

The Agricultural and Processed Food Products Export Development Authority (APEDA) was established by the Government of India under the Agricultural and Processed Food Products Export Development Authority Act passed by the Parliament in December, 1985. In accordance with the Agricultural and Processed Food Products Export Development Authority Act, 1985, (2 of 1986) the following functions have been assigned to the Authority. Development of industries relating to the scheduled products for export by way of providing financial assistance or otherwise for undertaking surveys and feasibility studies, participation in enquiry capital through joint ventures and other relief and subsidy schemes;

Functions of APEDA

1. Registration of persons as exporters of the scheduled products on payment of such fees as may be prescribed;
2. Fixing of standards and specifications for the scheduled products for the purpose of exports;
3. Carrying out inspection of meat and meat products in slaughter houses, processing plants, storage premises, conveyances or other places where such products are kept or handled for the purpose of ensuring the quality of such products;
4. Improving of packaging of the Scheduled products;
5. Improving of marketing of the Scheduled products outside India;
6. Promotion of export oriented production and development of the Scheduled products;
7. Collection of statistics from the owners of factories or establishments engaged in the production, processing, packaging, marketing or export of the scheduled products or from such other persons as may be prescribed on any matter relating to the scheduled products and publication of the statistics so collected or of any portions thereof or extracts there from;

5) Subsidy for the Marketing of Marine Products

The growing population resource imbalances have forced humans to explore the newer avenues to meet their needs. In this connection, people have been looking for sea foods. India with a large area exposed to sea has equally huge potential to reap the benefits be it domestic needs or earning revenue from export. Export of marine products plays a vital role in fisheries development in India by providing employment and income to millions engaged in fisheries, aquaculture, processing and allied activities. During the first year of the 11th Five Year Plan the Government has approved introduction of some new schemes to be implemented through MPEDA to boost export of marine products from India and also to provide assistance to the fish farmers / exporters / processors.

Fiscal Benefits

1) Exemption from Sales Tax

All the exporter or importer should register with local sales tax office at their jurisdiction. In order to claim any benefit under sales tax authorities, the registration of the company is mandatory. No sales tax is involved under sales. Any raw material is purchased for producing the product, which is exclusively for export purpose, the supplier is exempted from sales tax as the material supplied is for export purpose. Import or procurement of all types of goods including capital goods specified by the government is free of duty.

2) Exemption from Income Tax Import Facilitation for Exports Purpose

The units in Special Economic Zones are eligible for deduction under Section 10A of Income-tax Act, 1961 provides for deduction to the extent of 100% of profit and gains for 5 consecutive assessment year and thereafter to the extent of 50% of the profit and gains for a further period of 2 assessment year and for the next 3 consecutive assessment year, so much of the amount not exceeding 50% of the profits as is debited to the P/L account of the previous year. The units of 100% EOU are entitled for deduction under Section 10B of Income-tax Act, 1961 for relief from Income-tax burden for a period of 10 consecutive assessment year.

3) Export Promotion Capital Goods Scheme-EPCG

It is a special type of incentive given to the EPCG license holder. Capital goods imported under are subject to actual user condition and the same cannot be transferred /sold till the fulfillment of export obligation specified in the license. In order to ensure that the capital goods imported under EPCG Scheme, the license holder is required to produce certificate from the jurisdictional Central Excise Authority (CEA) or Chartered Engineer (CE) confirming installation of such capital goods in the declared premises. Under Export Promotion Capital Goods (EPCG) scheme, a license holder can import capital goods such as plant, machinery, equipment, components and spare parts of the machinery at concessional rate of customs duty of 5% and without CVD and special duty.

4) Duty Exemption Scheme–DES

The Duty Exemption Scheme enables import of inputs required for export production. The Duty Remission Scheme enables post export replenishment/ remission of duty on inputs used in the export product. These schemes are mostly available on those imported product, which will be latter on used for manufacturing of goods meant for export. This not only stimulates the industrial growth and development but also brings the foreign currency during the final export process. The following are some of the important import incentives offered by the Government of India, which significantly reduce the effective tax rates for the import companies:

5) 100% EOU /EPZ Unit / SEZ / STP/EHTP

a. 100% Export Oriented Unit

The Export Promotion Council for EOUs and SEZs (EPCES) has been set- up to service the export promotional needs of 100% Export Oriented Units (EOUs), Special Economic Zone (SEZ) Units and Agri Economic Zones in the country. EPCES represents EOU/SEZ Sector, which has over 2900 EOUs/SEZ Units, spread all over the country. The export earnings by this sector in

2005-06 is Rs. 59,967/- crore (US $ 13.84 billion) with a contribution of 13.19% in national exports. In the decade 1996-97 to 2005-06, exports from EOU/SEZ Sector has shown an average growth rate of 18.24%. This shows the potential of EOU/SEZ Scheme. This Council is a multi-product and scheme specific Export Promotion Council. The EOUs/SEZ Units cover major industrial sectors, like Textiles, Garments & Yarn, Food & Agro Products, Electronics & Software, Chemical, Engineering, Minerals, Granite, etc.

Objectives

The objectives of the Council are:

1. To promote exports from India and to earn more foreign exchange for the country.
2. To facilitate interaction between the exporting community and government both at the Central and State level.
3. To canalize financial assistance rendered by the Central Government to members
4. For assisting their export market development efforts.
5. To collaborate with other Export Promotion Councils/Export Promotion

Activities

The main activities of the Council are:

1. Providing financial assistance to EOUs/SEZ Units through Market Development Assistance for export promotion activities abroad.
2. Organising Open Houses/Seminars/Workshops in different states of the country for resolving their problems and eliciting suggestions for policy making by Government.
3. Taking up issues affecting EOUs/SEZ Units with various Ministries like Commerce, Finance, CBEC, CBDT, RBI, State Governments etc.
4. Participating in trade fairs/exhibitions in India and abroad.
5. Informing members about latest developments and changes in the national and international trade scenario.
6. Publishing a quarterly 'EPCES News' focusing on marketing strategies, international scene, latest provisions and procedures relating to Export-Import, Customs & Excise, Investment Opportunities etc.
7. Bringing out publications for use within India and abroad.
8. Organising buyer-seller meets with EOUs and SEZ Units for the promotion of exports.

b. Export Processing Zones (EPZ)

Many developing nations are trying to transform their economies by integrating themselves into the global supply chain. This means moving away from an import centric economy to one based on exports. One tool which is used by many nations is Export Processing Zones (EPZ). These are selected areas in a country that will attract foreign investment to create jobs, expand the industrial base, introduce technology, as well as create backward linkages between the zones and the domestic economy. The EPZ will have some resources that can attract investment such as natural resources, cheap skilled labor, or logistical advantages. Nations can also encourage investment in the EPZ by offering expedited licensing or building permits, minimal customs regulations, duty free tax incentives, such as a ten year tax holiday, and developing infrastructure to investor's requirements.

Advantages of the Export Processing Zone

With over 130 nations providing EPZ's within their borders, the advantages of creating EPZ's appear to be very clear for developing countries. The obvious benefits include the increase in foreign exchange through increased exports, job creation, foreign direct investment (FDI) to the host country, the introduction of technology into the country, and generating backward linkages from the EPZ to the domestic economy. The overall benefits to the host country are not clearly measurable as there is the initial development costs of creating the infrastructure for the EPZ, as well as the tax incentives offered to foreign investment.

Disadvantages of the Export Processing Zone

Many governments that have created EPZ's have acted against labor movement activities within EPZ's. The various restrictions on labor movements that governments have taken include a total or partial ban on trade union activities, restriction of the scope of collective bargaining, and banning trade union organizers. Most recently in Bangladesh the governments policy of banning unions has only softened after the building collapse that killed over 1100 workers.

Unsafe working conditions are a negative factor that are often associated with EPZ's. Workers are expected to work long hours in physically dangerous conditions, including excessive noise and heat, unsafe manufacturing equipment, and un inspected buildings. With no access to union representation, there is little that is done to change the situation in some factories. As more and more EPZ's are created, there is an incentive to keep costs as low as possible to be competitive against other developing nations. This means that the workers continue to suffer the consequences of unsafe working conditions.

c. Special Economic Zones

In order to overcome the shortcomings experienced on account of the multiplicity of controls and clearances; absence of world-class infrastructure, and an unstable fiscal regime and with a view to attract larger foreign investments in India, the Special Economic Zones (SEZs) Policy was announced in April 2000. It is a designated area in countries that possess special economic regulations that are different from other areas in the same country. These regulations tend to contain measures that are conducive to foreign direct investment. Conducting business in a SEZ usually means that a company will receive tax incentives and the opportunity to pay lower tariffs.

The major incentives and facilities available to SEZ developers

- Exemption from customs/excise duties for development of SEZs for authorized operations approved by the BOA.
- Income Tax exemption on income derived from the business of development of the SEZ in a block of 10 years in 15 years under Section 80-IAB of the Income Tax Act.
- Exemption from minimum alternate tax under Section 115 JB of the Income Tax Act.
- Exemption from dividend distribution tax under Section 115O of the Income Tax Act.
- Exemption from Central Sales Tax (CST).
- Exemption from Service Tax (Section 7, 26 and Second Schedule of the SEZ Act)

The incentives and facilities offered to the units in SEZs

1. Duty free import/domestic procurement of goods for development, operation and maintenance of SEZ units
2. 100% Income Tax exemption on export income for SEZ units under Section 10AA of the Income Tax Act for first 5 years, 50% for next 5 years thereafter and 50% of the ploughed back export profit for next 5 years.
3. Exemption from minimum alternate tax under section 115JB of the Income Tax Act.
4. External commercial borrowing by SEZ units upto US $ 500 million in a year without any maturity restriction through recognized banking channels.
5. Exemption from Central Sales Tax.
6. Exemption from Service Tax.
7. Single window clearance for Central and State level approvals.
8. Exemption from State sales tax and other levies as extended by the respective State Governments.

d. Software Technology Park [STP] Scheme

Software Technology Park[STP] Scheme is a 100% export oriented scheme for undertaking software development for export using data communication links or in the form of physical media including export of professional services. The scheme was set up to contribute to the prosperity of the national economy through promotion of exports from the Software & services Industry by facilitating all the statutory services of the Govt., strengthening the Communication Infrastructure and by increasing the quality consciousness in the Industry.

The Benefits under the STP

1. Approvals are given under single window clearance mechanism.
2. An STP project may be set up anywhere in India.
3. Jurisdictional Directors have the powers to approve import of capital goods (net of taxes) not more than US$ 20 million.
4. 100% Foreign equity is permitted.
5. All the imports of Hardware & Software in the STP units are completely duty free, import of second hand capital goods also permitted.
6. Re-Export of capital goods are permitted.
7. Simplified Minimum Export Performance norms

e. Electronic Hardware Technology Park (EHTP)

For encouraging exports of electronic hardware items including hard disk drives, computers, television, etc., such parks have been developed by the Ministry of Communications & Information Technology. An Electronic Hardware Technology Park (EHTP) may be an individual unit by itself or a unit located in an area designated as Electronic Hardware Technology Park Complex. As in the case of STP Scheme, the Electronic Hardware Technology Park Scheme is also administered by the Ministry of Communications & Information Technology. An Electronic Hardware Technology Park can also be set up by the Central Government, State Government, public or private sector undertakings or any combination of them. The entire production of an Electronic Hardware Technology Park is to be exported to hard currency areas except sales in the Domestic Tariff Areas, subject to the limits set down.

Benefits Granted to Electronic Hardware Technology Park

An Electronic Hardware Technology Park may import free of duty capital goods, raw materials, components and other related inputs.

1. An EHTP unit may bunch the products manufactured by it for sale in the Domestic Tariff Area (DTA) with its entitlement.
2. EHTPs are duty free and bonded areas and customs exemptions are extended accordingly.
3. An EHTP may gear up to 100 per cent foreign equity.
4. Supplies that are effected in DTAs under global tender conditions and payment in forex are also considered as part of relinquishment of export obligation.
5. Supplies made by DTAs to an EHTP unit will be regarded as deemed exports and is entitled to benefits under the Foreign Trade Policy. To get this benefit, goods have to be produced in the country and the supplies have to be made against a letter of authority issued by an officer designated in this behalf of the STPI, Government of India.
6. An EHTP unit may be setup for both software and hardware in an integrated manner.
7. EHTP unit may purchase indigenous goods free of excise duty.
8. EHTP unit may sell Goods/Services in DTA up to 50% of FOB value of exports, subject to fulfillment of positive NFE as per the policy & payment of applicable duties.

Export Financing

Introduction

The term 'export financing' refers to credit facilities and techniques of payments at the pre-shipment and post-shipment stages. Export finance whether short-term or medium term, is provided exclusively by the Indian and foreign commercial banks which are the members of the Foreign Exchange Dealers Association. The Reserve Bank of India (RBI) and the Industrial Development Bank of India (IDBI) provide refinance facilities to the commercial banks. Export-Import Bank of India (commonly known as EXIM Bank) also extends finance to exporters and to overseas projects abroad joint ventures and construction projects abroad. Exporters naturally want to get paid as quickly as possible, while importers usually prefer to delay payment until they have received or resold the goods. Because of the intense competition for export markets, being able to offer attractive payment terms customary in the trade is often necessary to make a sale. Exporters should be aware of the many financing options open to them so that they choose the most acceptable one to both the buyer and the seller. The most important financing options open to exporters are as under:

- Pre-shipment finance
- Post-shipment finance

Pre-shipment Finance

Pre-shipment finance refers to the financial assistance provided to the exporters before actual shipment of goods. Pre-shipment finance is provided to the exporters for the purposes like purchase of raw materials, their processing and converting into finished goods and packaging them.

Pre Shipment Finance is issued by a financial institution when the seller want the payment of the goods before shipment. Pre-shipment credits are granted by the banks under concessional rates of interest at 7.5 per cent. Credit can be extended up to a maximum period of 6 months.

The main objectives behind preshipment finance or pre export finance are to enable exporter to:

- Procure raw materials.
- Carry out manufacturing process.
- Provide a secure warehouse for goods and raw materials.

- Process and pack the goods.
- Ship the goods to the buyers.
- Meet other financial cost of the business.

Packing credit facility can be provided to an exporter on production of the following evidences to the bank:

Formal application for release the packing credit with undertaking to the effect that the exporter would be ship the goods within stipulated due date and submit the relevant shipping documents to the banks within prescribed time limit.

Firm order or irrevocable L/C or original cable/fax/telex message exchange between the exporter and the buyer.

Licence issued by DGFT if the goods to be exported fall under the restricted or canalized category. If the item falls under quota system, proper quota allotment proof needs to be submitted.

The confirmed order received from the overseas buyer should reveal the information about the full name and address of the overseas buyer, description quantity and value of goods (FOB or CIF), destination port and the last date of payment.

Eligibility

Pre shipment credit is only issued to that exporter who has the export order in his own name. However, as an exception, financial institution can also grant credit to a third party manufacturer or supplier of goods who does not have export orders in their own name. In this case some of the responsibilities of meeting the export requirements have been out sourced to them by the main exporter. In other cases where the export order is divided between two more than two exporters, pre shipment credit can be shared between them

Quantum of Finance

The Quantum of Finance is granted to an exporter against the LC or an expected order. The only guideline principle is the concept of Need Based Finance.

Banks determine the percentage of margin, depending on factors such as:

- The nature of Order.
- The nature of the commodity.
- The capability of exporter to bring in the requisite contribution.

Different Stages of Pre Shipment Finance

Appraisal and Sanction of Limits

1.   Before making any an allowance for Credit facilities banks need to check the different aspects like product profile, political and economic details about country. Apart from these things, the bank also looks in to the status report of the prospective buyer, with whom the exporter proposes to do the business. To check all these information, banks can seek the help of institution like ECGC or International consulting agencies like Dun and Brad street etc.

The Bank extended the packing credit facilities after ensuring the following"

- The exporter is a regular customer, a bona fide exporter and has a goods standing in the market.
- Whether the exporter has the necessary license and quota permit (as mentioned earlier) or not.
- Whether the country with which the exporter wants to deal is under the list of Restricted Cover Countries (RCC) or not.

Disbursement of Pre Shipment Finance

Once the proper sanctioning of the documents is done, bank ensures whether exporter has executed the list of documents mentioned earlier or not. Disbursement is normally allowed when all the documents are properly executed. Sometimes an exporter is not able to produce the export order at time of availing packing credit. So, in these cases, the bank provides a special packing credit facility and is known as Running Account Packing. The quantum of finance is fixed depending on the FOB value of contract /LC or the domestic values of goods, whichever is found to be lower. Normally insurance and freight charged are considered at a later stage, when the goods are ready to be shipped. In this case disbursals are made only in stages and if possible not in cash. The payments are made directly to the supplier by drafts/bankers/cheques. The bank decides the duration of packing credit depending upon the time required by the exporter for processing of goods. The maximum duration of packing credit period is 180 days,however bank may provide a further 90 days extension on its own discretion, without referring to RBI.

Follow up of Pre Shipment Finance

Exporter needs to submit stock statement giving all the necessary information about the stocks. It is then used by the banks as a guarantee for securing the packing credit in advance. Bank also decides the rate of submission of these stocks. Apart from this, authorized dealers (banks) also physically inspect the stock at regular intervals.

Liquidation of Pre Shipment Finance

Packing Credit Advance needs be liquidated out of as the export proceeds of the relevant shipment, thereby converting preshipment credit into post shipment credit. This liquidation can also be done by the payment receivable from the Government of India and includes the duty drawback, payment from the Market Development Fund (MDF) of the Central Government or from any other relevant source. In case if the export does not take place then the entire advance can also be recovered at a certain interest rate.

RBI has allowed some flexibility in to this regulation under which substitution of commodity or buyer can be allowed by a bank without any reference to RBI. Hence in effect the packing credit advance may be repaid by proceeds from export of the same or another commodity to the same or another buyer. However, bank need to ensure that the substitution is commercially necessary and unavoidable. Bank considers a packing credit as an overdue, if the borrower fails to liquidate the packing credit on the due date. And, if the condition persists then the bank takes the necessary step to recover its dues as per normal recovery procedure.

Types of Pre Shipment Finance

1. Pre-Shipment Credit to Sub Supplier

Packing Credit can only be shared on the basis of disclaimer between the Export Order Holder (EOH) and the manufacturer of the goods. This disclaimer is normally issued by the EOH in order to indicate that he is not availing any credit facility against the portion of the order transferred in the name of the manufacturer. On supply of goods, the L/C opening bank will pay to the sub supplier's bank against the inland documents received on the basis of the inland L/C opened by them. The final responsibility of EOH is to export the goods as per guidelines. Any delay in export order can bring EOH to penal provisions that can be issued anytime.

The main objective of this method is to cover only the first stage of production cycles, and is not to be extended to cover supplies of raw material etc. Running account facility is not granted to sub suppliers. In case the EOH is a trading house, the facility is available commencing from the manufacturer to whom the order has been passed by the trading house. Banks however, ensure that there is no double financing and the total period of packing credit does not exceed the actual cycle of production of the commodity.

2. Running Account Facility

It is a special facility under which a bank has right to grant preshipment advance for export to the exporter of any origin. Sometimes banks also extent these facilities depending upon the good track record of the exporter. In return the exporter needs to produce the letter of credit / firms export order within a given period of time.

3. Preshipment Credit in Foreign Currency (PCFC)

Authorised dealers are permitted to extend Preshipment Credit in Foreign Currency (PCFC) with an objective of making the credit available to the exporters at internationally competitive price. This is considered as an added advantage under which credit is provided in foreign currency in order to facilitate the purchase of raw material after fulfilling the basic export orders. The exporter has freedom to avail PCFC in convertible currencies like USD, Pound, Sterling, Euro, Yen etc. However, the risk associated with the cross currency truncation is that of the exporter.

4. Packing Credit Facilities to Deemed Exports

Deemed exports made to multilateral funds aided projects and programmes, under orders secured through global tenders for which payments will be made in free foreign exchange, are eligible for concessional rate of interest facility both at pre and post supply stages.

5. Packing Credit Facilities for Consulting Services

In case of consultancy services, exports do not involve physical movement of goods out of Indian Customs Territory. In such cases, Preshipment finance can be provided by the bank to allow the exporter to mobilize resources like technical personnel and training them.

6. Advance Against Cheque/Drafts Received as Advance Payment

Where exporters receive direct payments from abroad by means of cheques/drafts etc. the bank may grant export credit at concessional rate to the exporters of goods track record, till the time of realization of the proceeds of the cheques or draft etc. The Banks however, must satisfy themselves that the proceeds are against an export order.

Post-shipment Finance

Post Shipment Finance is a kind of loan provided by a financial institution to an exporter or seller against a shipment that has already been made. This type of export finance is granted from the date of extending the credit after shipment of the goods to the realization date of the exporter proceeds. Exporters don't wait for the importer to deposit the funds. Post shipment finance is meant to finance export sales receivable after the date of shipment of goods to the date of realization of exports proceeds. In cases of deemed exports, it is extended to finance receivable against supplies made to designated agencies. Post shipment finances are provided against evidence of shipment of goods or supplies made to the importer or seller or any other designated agency.

Post shipment finance can be secured or unsecured. Since the finance is extended against evidence of export shipment and bank obtains the documents of title of goods, the finance is normally self liquidating. In that case it involves advance against undrawn balance, and is usually unsecured in nature. Further, the finance is mostly a funded advance. In few cases, such as financing of project exports, the issue of guarantee (retention money guarantees) is involved and the financing is not funded in nature.

Quantum of Finance

As a quantum of finance, post shipment finance can be extended up to 100% of the invoice value of goods. In special cases, where the domestic value of the goods increases the value of the exporter order, finance for a price difference can also be extended and the price difference is covered by the government. This type of finance is not extended in case of preshipment stage. Banks can also finance undrawn balance. In such cases banks are free to stipulate margin requirements as per their usual lending norm.

Period of Finance

Post shipment finance can be off short terms or long term, depending on the payment terms offered by the exporter to the overseas importer. In case of cash exports, the maximum period allowed for realization of exports proceeds is six months from the date of shipment. Concessive rate of interest is available for a highest period of 180 days, opening from the date of surrender of documents. Usually, the documents need to be submitted within 21days from the date of shipment.

Types of Post Shipment Finance

The Post Shipment Finance can be Classified as under

- Export Bills purchased/discounted.
- Export Bills negotiated
- Advance against export bills sent on collection basis.
- Advance against export on consignment basis
- Advance against undrawn balance on exports
- Advance against claims of Duty Drawback.

1. Export Bills Purchased/ Discounted.(DP & DA Bills)

Export bills (Non L/C Bills) is used in terms of sale contract/ order may be discounted or purchased by the banks. It is used in indisputable international trade transactions and the proper limit has to be sanctioned to the exporter for purchase of export bill facility.

2. Export Bills Negotiated (Bill under L/C)

The risk of payment is less under the LC, as the issuing bank makes sure the payment. The risk is further reduced, if a bank guarantees the payments by confirming the LC. Because of the inborn security available in this method, banks often become ready to extend the finance against bills under LC.

3. Advance Against Export Bills Sent on Collection Basis

Bills can only be sent on collection basis, if the bills drawn under LC have some discrepancies. Sometimes exporter requests the bill to be sent on the collection basis, anticipating the strengthening of foreign currency. Banks may allow advance against these collection bills to an exporter with a concessional rates of interest depending upon the transit period in case of DP Bills and transit period plus usance period in case of usance bill. The transit period is from the date of acceptance of the export documents at the banks branch for collection and not from the date of advance.

4. Advance against Export on Consignments Basis

Bank may choose to finance when the goods are exported on consignment basis at the risk of the exporter for sale and eventual payment of sale proceeds to him by the consignee. However, in this case bank instructs the overseas bank to deliver the document only against trust receipt /undertaking to deliver the sale proceeds by specified date, which should be within the prescribed date even if according to the practice in certain trades a bill for part of the estimated value is drawn in advance against the exports. In case of export through approved Indian owned warehouses abroad the times limit for realization is 15 months.

5. Advance Against Undrawn Balance

It is a very common practice in export to leave small part undrawn for payment after adjustment due to difference in rates, weight, quality etc. Banks do finance against the undrawn balance, if undrawn balance is in conformity with the normal level of balance left undrawn in the particular line of export, subject to a maximum of 10 percent of the export value. An undertaking is also obtained from the exporter that he will, within 6 months from due date of payment or the date of shipment of the goods, whichever is earlier surrender balance proceeds of the shipment.

6. Advance Against Claims of Duty Drawback

Duty Drawback is a type of discount given to the exporter in his own country. This discount is given only, if the in-house cost of production is higher in relation to international price. This type of financial support helps the exporter to fight successfully in the international markets. In such a situation, banks grants advances to exporters at lower rate of interest for a maximum period of 90 days. These are granted only if other types of export finance are also extended to the exporter by the same bank. After the shipment, the exporters lodge their claims, supported by the relevant documents to the relevant government authorities. These claims are processed and eligible amount is disbursed after making sure that the bank is authorized to receive the claim amount directly from the concerned government authorities.

Documents in Foreign Trade

More than two dozen commercial and regulatory documents are involved in the pre-shipment stage of export transactions. These include 17 commercial documents and 9 regulatory documents.

Commercial Documents

The commercial documents are those which, by customs of trade, are required for affecting physical transfer of goods and their title from the exporter to the importer and the realisation of export sale proceeds. Shipping order and Bill of exchange could not be brought within the fold of the aligned

The commercial documents are those which, by customs of trade, are required for affecting physical transfer of goods and their title from the exporter to the importer and the realisation of export sale proceeds. Shipping order and Bill of exchange could not be brought within the fold of the aligned documentation system because of their very different data elements and having very little in common with other commercial documents.

The commercial documents may be classified into

a. Principal documents
b. Auxiliary documents

a) Principal Export Documents

The exporter is required to send the following eight documents to the importer. These are known as the principal export documents:

1. Commercial Invoice

It is a document required by customs to determine true value of the imported goods, for assessment of duties and taxes. A commercial invoice must be used when the goods shipped reflect a commercial transaction and are for permanent export. A commercial invoice must identify the buyer and seller, and clearly indicate the date and terms of sale, quantity, weight and/or volume of the shipment, type of packaging, complete description of goods, unit value and total value, and insurance, shipping and other charges.

A commercial invoice must contain the following information:

- Full name and postal address of the seller and the buyer with contact details
- Number and date of issue of commercial invoice and the number of the order
- Marks, numbers, number, kind and gross weight of packages

- Trade description of goods in plain language and in sufficient detail
- Quantity of the goods and their gross and net weight
- Price of goods and currency
- Country of origin of the goods
- Transport route and means of transport used
- Reference to sales contract number and date
- One original signed copy of the invoice is required, as well as a total of five copies.

2. Packing List

A packing list is a document that includes details about the contents of a package. The packing list is intended to let transport agencies, government authorities, and customers know the contents of the package. These details help each of these parties handle the package accordingly. A packing list is expresses the contents of a package, along with details about the quantity, description, and weight of these contents. Content pricing is not included. A packing list is created by the seller and sent to where the goods are located in order to have an accurate tally of the sent goods. Once the goods have been tallied and packed, the list is sent along with them to their destination. A packing list is a catalogue of all the articles that are included in a package that has been shipped from one place to another. A packing list is helpful for confirming the number of items and make sure that nothing has been misplaced.

3. Bill of Lading

Bill of lading is one of the most important documents in the shipping process. To ship any goods, a bill of lading is required and acts as a receipt and a contract. A legal document between the shipper of a particular good and the carrier detailing the type, quantity and destination of the good being carried. The bill of lading also serves as a receipt of shipment when the good is delivered to the predetermined destination. This document must accompany the shipped goods, no matter the form of transportation, and must be signed by an authorized representative from the carrier, shipper and receiver. Bill of lading (BOL) is one of the most important documents in the shipping process. A completed BOL legally shows that the carrier has received the freight as described and is obligated to deliver that freight in good condition to the consignee. The information in the bill of lading is critical as it directs the actions of personnel all along the route of the shipment - where it's going, the piece count, how it's billed, and how it's to be handled on the dock and trailers. It could be on a prepaid or collect basis. The consignee has to check whether the shipment is collect on delivery which means that the driver will collect the cost of the merchandise on delivery of the freight.

4. Combined Transport Document

It is shipping contract for transportation of goods via two or more means of transport. It indicates the name of the carrier and be signed by the carrier or a named agent for or on behalf of the carrier, or - the master or a named agent for or on behalf of the master. It Indicate the place of dispatch, taking in charge or shipment and the place of final destination, terms and conditions of carriage or make reference to another source containing the terms and conditions of carriage. Combined transport is a form of transport whereby goods in one and the same loading unit or road vehicle, using successively two or more modes of transport without handling the goods themselves in changing modes. Combined transport is a transport where the major part of the journey is by rail, inland waterways or sea, and any initial and/ or final legs carried out by road are as short as possible.

5. Certificate of Inspection/Quality Control

When shipping high-value products or when you are dealing with a very conscientious customer, an inspection certificate might be requested. An inspection certificate provides proof that what you are shipping is, in fact, what the customer ordered, and is also of good quality. An inspection certificate can be furnished directly to a buyer, a buyer's government or direct to a buyer's bank. In the case of presenting to a buyer's bank, that is precipitated by the request of a Letter of Credit payment transaction that spells out specifically an inspection certificate is required in order to fulfill payment obligations. Generally, a manufacturer furnishes the certificate or the report. Quality control is a process by which entities review the quality of all factors involved in production. Quality control emphasizes testing of products to uncover defects and reporting to management who make the decision to allow or deny product release, whereas quality assurance attempts to improve and stabilize production.

6. Insurance Certificate

A certificate of insurance is often demanded in situations where liability and large losses are a concern. A document issued by an insurance company/broker that is used to verify the existence of insurance coverage under specific conditions granted to listed individuals. More specifically, the document lists the effective date of the policy, the type of insurance coverage purchased, and the types and dollar amount of applicable liability.

7. Certificate of origin

A Certificate of Origin (CO) is an important international trade document attesting that goods in a particular export shipment are wholly obtained, produced, manufactured or processed in a particular country. COs also constitute a declaration by the exporter. Virtually every country in the world considers the origin of imported goods when determining what duty will be assessed on the goods or, in some cases, whether the goods may be legally imported at all. There are two types of Certificate of Origin namely ordinary and preferential certificate of origin. The ordinary COs certifies that the country of origin of a particular product does not qualify for any preferential treatment. Preferential COs enables products to enjoy tariff reduction or exemption when they are exported to countries extending these privileges. In most countries, chambers of commerce are the key agent in the delivery of certificates of origin. However, in some countries, this privilege may also be extended to other bodies such as ministries or customs authorities.

8. Bills of Exchange

A bill of exchange is the most often used form of payment in local and international trade, and has a long history. A written, unconditional order by one party (the drawer) to another (the drawee) to pay a certain sum, either immediately (a sight bill) or on a fixed date (a term bill), for payment of goods and/ or services received. The drawee accepts the bill by signing it, thus converting it into a post-dated check and a binding contract. A bill of exchange contains: (1) The term bill of exchange inserted in the body of the instrument and expressed in the language employed in drawing up the instrument. (2) An unconditional order to pay a determinate sum of money. (3) The name of the person who is to pay (drawee). (4) A statement of the time of payment. (5) A statement of the place where payment is to be made. (6) The name of the person to whom or to whose order payment is to be made. (7) A statement of the date and of the place where the bill is issued. (8) The signature of the person who issues the bill (drawer).

9. Shipment Advice

Shipment Advice is a note sent to a buying exporter that their cargo is on its way. A copy of both the invoice and packing slip is also sent sometimes. Advice of Shipment is a notice sent to a local or foreign buyer advising that shipment has gone forward and contains details of packing, routing, etc. A copy of the invoice is often enclosed and, if desired, a copy of the bill of lading.

Auxiliary Documents

The remaining documents are known as the auxiliary documents. They are:

1. Proforma Invoice

Proforma invoice is an abridged or estimated invoice sent by a seller to a buyer in advance of a shipment or delivery of goods. It notes the kind and quantity of goods, their value, and other important information such as weight and transportation charges. Pro forma invoices are commonly used as preliminary invoices with a quotation, or for customs purposes in importation. They differ from a normal invoice in not being a demand or request for payment.

2. Intimation for Inspection

It is a critical appraisal involving examination, measurement, testing, gauging, and comparison of materials or items. An inspection determines if the material or item is in proper quantity and condition, and if it conforms to the applicable or specified requirements. Inspection is generally divided into three categories: (1) Receiving inspection, (2) In-process inspection, and (3) Final inspection.

3. Shipping Instructions

Shipping instructions is a document sent by an exporter giving details of how goods are to be shipped and delivered. This is also called shipper's letter of instruction that directs a carrier in preparing shipping documents for the subject shipment, and provides for the necessary declarations.

4. Insurance Declaration

Insurance declarations contain all of the basic information that defines the policy. These declarations include the name of the insured, the amount of coverage and the name, description and location of the item or items being covered.

5. Shipping Order

Shipping order is a document used by a business to specify what items are to be transferred from a storage location or warehouse to what person and to what new location. A shipping order typically is sent along with a shipment of goods so that the person receiving them can verify that the document correctly reflects the items that they actually received.

6. Mate Receipt

A mate receipt is a receipt Issued by the Commanding Office of the ship when the cargo is loaded on the ship, and contains information about the name of the vessel, berth, date of shipment, description of packages, marks and numbers, condition of the cargo at the time of receipt on board the ship, etc. The mate receipt is first handed over to the Port Trust authorities so that all the port dues may be paid by the exporter. After paying all the port dues, the merchant or the agent may collect the mate receipt from the Port Trust authorities. The bill of lading is prepared by the shipping agent after the mate receipt has been obtained.

7. Application for Certificate of Origin

The Indian Chamber of Commerce (ICC) is authorized by the Directorate General of Foreign Trade and Ministry of Commerce, Govt. of India to issue Non-preferential Certificate of Origin to the exporters. ICC has been efficiently providing this service at a nominal cost. Special discounts are available for ICC members. The exporters seeking Certificate of Origin have to execute an indemnity bond in favour of the ICC before they can avail of this service for the first time. Thereafter preprinted certificate of origin forms can be obtained from the ICC office. Exporters can get the certificate of origin and allied documents duly attested and signed by one of the authorized signatories of ICC by paying the requisite service charges.

8. Letter to the Bank for Collection/Negotiation of Documents

Once the goods are dispatched to foreign destination, the exporter should approach his bank with a formal letter called 'letter to bank', requesting the bank to realize the export bills from the overseas buyer. It is obligatory for an exporter to hand over the relative documents within 21 days of shipment to his bank for onward dispatch to the overseas correspondent bank who will arrange payment of the same to his banker. Thus, the legal requirement is that the payment against the export should be realized through an authorized foreign exchange dealer within 6 months of date of shipment. These documents are handed over to the bank with a request either to negotiate the documents if the same are drawn under the letter of credit or to purchase the documents where the bank has granted pre-shipment facility to the exporter or has sanctioned post-shipment limit for purchase of export bills or to collect the bills with or without any advance against the security of these bills.

Regulatory Documents

Regulatory pre-shipment export documents are those which have been prescribed by different Government departments/bodies in compliance of the requirements of various rules and regulations under relevant laws governing export trade such as export inspection, foreign exchange regulations, export trade control, customs etc. There are 9 regulatory documents associated with the pre-shipment stage of an export transaction and are as follows:

1. Gate Pass-V, Gate Pass II - Prescribed by Central Excise Authorities

A GP form is a gate pass for the removal of excisable goods from a factory or warehouse. Form GP 1 is used for the removal of excisable goods on payment of duty and form GP 2 is used for the removal of excisable goods without payment of duty. Form C is to be used for applying for rebate of duty on the excisable goods (other than vegetable, non-essential oils and tea) exported by sea. It is to be submitted in triplicate to the Collector of Central Excises.

2. AR4/AR4A Form - Prescribed by Central Excise Authorities

These forms are meant for applying for the removal of excisable goods for export by sea / post. Form A.R.-4 is used for applying for excise inspection at the factory and form A.R.-4A is used when goods are to be exported under a claim for rebate of excise duty or under bond. Shipping Bill/Bill of Export - Prescribed by Central Excise Authorities

It is a customs document used where drawback is claimed, such as on goods exported or on dutiable goods transshipped or re-exported from a bonded warehouse. It serves basically as a statistical record for export of goods, export of duty free goods, for export of dutiable goods and for export of goods under claim for duty drawback.

3. Export Application/Dock Challan as prescribed by Port Trust

A printed form filled in all respect is submitted to dock authorities along with goods is called dock Challan. This is prepared in duplicate. One copy is regained by dock authorities and the second copy is returned to the exporter which is known as dock receipt.

4. Receipt for Payment of Port Charges

Maintenance of port in efficient manner is a prerequisite for effective foreign trade for any country. Keeping this in view, the exporter pays some charges for the use of port facilities and this one of the important regulatory documents.

5. Vehicle Ticket

A vehicle ticket is prepared by the exporter and includes details of the export cargo in tones of the shipper's name, the numb of packages, the shipping bill number, the port of destination and the number of the vehicle carrying the cargo. The driver of the vehicle carrying cargo should present it to the gate warden/ inspector/keeper along with other shipping and port documents. The gate keeper/warden/ inspector, after satisfying himself allow it to pass the gate.

6. Exchange Control Declaration as prescribed by RBI GR/PP Forms

Foreign exchange regulations in India require the exporter to fill several forms. There are four important types of forms, namely, GR\PP, VP\COD and SOFTEX form for export of computer software obtainable from the RBI or a bank authorised to deal the foreign exchange.

7. Freight Payment Certificate

It is a certificate showing that freight for the goods meant for export has been paid. It is a document that indicates that the freight for the consignment has been paid to the shipping company. It is a supplementary evidence to avail of the second bill of lading in case of the original has been lost.

8. Insurance Premium Payment Certificate

It is a document evidencing insurance has been taken out on the goods shipped. It also gives full details of the insurance cover. An insurance premium payment certificate certifies that the shipment has been insured under a given open policy and is to cover loss of or damage to the cargo while in transit.

Classification of Documents on the Basis of Needs & Requirements

A. Documents Related to Good

1. Invoice
2. Packing List/Note
3. Certificate of Origin

B. Documents Related to Shipment

1. Mate Receipt
2. Shipping Bill
3. Cart Ticket
4. Certificate of Measurement
5. Bill of Lading
6. Airway Bill (AWB)
7. Form B-X, for export by Post

C. Documents Related to Payments

Letter of Credit Bill of Exchange Trust Receipt

Letter of Hypothecation Bank Certificate of Payment

D. Document Related to Inspection

1. Certificate of Inspection

E. Documents Related to Excisable Goods

1.   GP Forms
2.   Form C
2.   AR-4/AR-4A Form

F. Documents Related to Foreign Exchange Regulations

1.   GR Forms
2.   PP Forms
3.   VP/COD Forms
4.   CNX Forms

Documents related to Goods

(I) Invoice

An invoice is the seller's bill for merchandise and contains particulars of goods, such as the price per unit at a particular location, quantity, total value, packing specifications, terms of sale, identification marks of the package, bill of lading number, name arid address of the importer, destination, name of the ship, etc. Some importing countries insist that the invoice should be signed by the importing country's consul located in the exporter's country. Such invoices signed by the consul are known as consular invoice. The main purpose of a consular invoice is to enable the authorities of the importing country to collect accurate information about the volume, value, quality, grade, source, etc., of its imports for purpose of assessing import duties and also for statistical purposes. The special invoice forms for various countries may be obtained from any Chamber of Commerce. Exporters may consult the respective Export Promotion Councils regarding the correct producers and invoice forms for different countries.

(II) Packing Note and List

The difference between a packing note and a packing list is that the packing note refers to the particulars of the contents of an individual pack, while the packing list is a consolidated statement of the contents of a number of cases or packs. A packing note should include the packing note number, the date of packing, the name and address of the exporter, the name and address of the importer, the order number, shipment per SS, bill of lading number and date, marking numbers, case number to which the note relates, and the contents of the goods in terms of quantity and weight. Apart from the details in the packing note, a packing list should also include item-wise details. No particular form has been prescribed for the packing note or packing list. Normal ten copies of the packing note/list should be prepared. The first is to be sent with the shipping documents, two copies in advance to the buyer, one to the shipping agent and the remaining retained by the exporter.

(III) Certificate of Origin

A certificate of origin, as the name indicates, is a certificate which specifies the country of the production of the goods. This certificate has also to be produced before clearance of goods and assessment of duty, for the customs law of the country may require this procedure. This certificate is a necessity where a country offers a preferential tariff to India and the former is to ensure that only goods of Indian origin benefit from such concession. A certificate of origin may be required when goods of a particular type from certain countries are banned. A certificate of origin form may be obtained from Chambers of Commerce, Export Promotion Councils, and various trade associations which have been authorised by the Government.

Documents Related To Shipment

(i) Mate Receipt

A mate receipt is a receipt Issued by the Commanding Office of the ship when the cargo is loaded on the ship, and contains information about the name of the vessel, berth, date of shipment, description of packages, marks and numbers, condition of the cargo at the time of receipt on board the ship, etc. The mate receipt is first handed over to the Port Trust authorities so that all the port dues may be paid by the exporter. After paying all the port dues, the merchant or the agent may collect the mate receipt from the Port Trust authorities. The bill of lading is prepared by the shipping agent after the mate receipt has been obtained.

(ii) Shipping Bill

The shipping bill is the main document on the basis of which the Customs' permission for export is given. The shipping bill contains particulars of the goods exported, the name of the vessel, master or agents, flag, the port at which goods are to be discharged, the country of final destination, the exporter's name and address, etc. It also contains details of the packages and the goods, such as number and description, marks and numbers, quantity details about each case, F.O.B. prices, real value as defined in die Sea Customs Act, whether Indian or foreign merchandise to be re-exported, total number of packages, their total weight and value, etc.

(iii) Cart Ticket

A cart ticket, also known as a cart chit, vehicle and gate pass which is prepared by the exporter and includes details of the export cargo in tones of the shipper's name, the numb of packages, the shipping bill number, the port of destination and the number of the vehicle carrying the cargo. The driver of the vehicle carrying cargo should present it to the gate warden/ inspector/keeper along with other shipping and port documents. The gate keeper/warden/ inspector, after satisfying himself allow it to pass the gate.

(iv) Certificate of Measurement

Freight is charged either on the basis of weight or measurement, when it is charged on the basis of weight, the weight declared by the shipper may be accepted. However, a certificate of measurement from die Indian Chamber of Commerce or other approved organisation may be obtained by the shipper and given to the shipping company for the calculation of the necessary freight. The certificate contains die name of the vessel, port and destination, the description of goods, the quantity, length, breadth, depth, etc., of the packages.

(v) Bill of Lading

The bill of lading is a document where in the shipping company gives its official receipts for the goods shipped in its vessel and at the same time contracts to carry them to the port of destination. It is also a document of title to the goods and, as such, is freely transferable by endorsement and delivery. A bill of lading is the acknowledgment of the receipt of the goods by the crew of the ship. A bill of lading serves three main purposes:

- As a document of title to the goods
- As a receipt from the shipping company; and
- As a contract for the transportation of goods.

Each shipping company has its own bill of lading. The exporter prepares the bill of lading in the forms obtained from the shipping company or from the agents of the shipping company. The information contained in the bill of lading includes the date and place of shipment, the name of the consignor, the name and destination of the vessel, the description, quality and destination of the goods, the masks and numbers, the invoice number and the date of export; the gross weight and net weight; the number of packages, the amount of freight, etc.

Whenever the carrier has to use other transport facilities, such as rail, road, or another steamship company in addition to his own the consignee's centre, the carrier issues a through or transshipment bill of lading. A bill of lading that has been held too long before it is passed on to a bank or the consignee is called a stale bill of lading. When freight is paid at the time of shipment or in advance, the bill of landing is marked, freight paid; if the freight is not paid and is to be collected from the consignee on the arrival of the goods, the bill of lading is marked, freight collect.

(vi) Airway Bill

An airway bill, also called, an air consignment note, is a receipt issued by an airline for the carriage of goods. As each shipping company has its own bill of lading, each airline has its own airway bill.

Documents Related To Payment

(a) Letter of Credit

A letter of credit is a document containing the guarantee of a bank to honour drafts drawn on it by an exporter, under certain conditions and up to certain amounts, provided that the beneficiary fulfils the stipulated conditions. For details of the letter of credit and the use of the letter of credit in financing foreign trade, see Annexure to the Chapter on Export Financing.

(b) Bill of Exchange

The Negotiable Instruments Act, 1881, defines the bill of exchange as "an instrument in writing containing an unconditional order, signed by the maker, directing a certain person to pay a certain sum of money only to or to the order of a certain person or to the bearer of the instrument." There are the following important types of bill of exchange:

(i) Sight Bill of Exchange

A sight or demand bill of exchange is one which is required to be paid by the drawee immediately on presentation of the bill.

(ii) Usance Bill of Exchanged

In case of the usance or time bill of exchange, there is maturity period called the tenor, and the payment is to be made only on the maturity of the bill. Generally speaking, the due date of payment of the usance bill is calculated from the date of presentation or sighting of the bill by the drawee. Such a bill is called after sight usance bill. But sometimes the date of maturity is calculated from the date of drawing of the bill. Such a bill is known as after date usance bill.

(iii) Clean Bill of Exchange

A bill of exchange not accompanied by the relative shipping documents is known as a clean bill of exchange. In respect of the clean bill of exchange, the documents are sent to the consignee directly, and he can take delivery of the goods on their arrival at the port of destination.

(iv) Documentary Bill of Exchange

A documentary bill of exchange is a bill of exchange accompanied by the relative shipping documents such as the bill of lading, marine insurance policy, commercial invoice, certificate of origin, etc. The documents accompanying the bill are delivered to the importer by the bank only upon either acceptance or payment of the bill. The former is called documents against acceptance and the later is called documents against payment. It is the documentary bill of exchange that is commonly used in foreign trade transactions.

(c) Trust Receipt

If the importer is unable to take possession of the documents by making the payment of the Document against Payment bill following the arrival of the goods, the merchandise may be made available to the importer by his bank under an arrangement whereby the importer signs a trust receipt. Under this arrangement, the importer is allowed to sell the imported goods by acting as an agent of the bank; but he retains ownership of the merchandise until (he importer has made full settlement; all sums received from the sale of goods must be credited to the bank until such settlement is made.

(d) Letter of Hypothecation

A letter of hypothecation is a document signed by the customer conveying to a banker the full ownership of goods at the port of destination in respect of which he has made advances either by loan or by acceptance or negotiation of bills of exchange. This is a sort of blanket document which any banker, who accepts bills, advances money or negotiates bills and shipping documents, demands from a customer to give him recourse on the bills and control of the documents. The letter of hypothecation pledges the documents of title with the banker as security for an advance and gives the bank power to sell the goods. If necessary, to insure them and to warehouse them at the customer's expense.

(e) Bank Certificate of Payment

It is a certificate issued by the negotiating bank of the exporter, certifying that the bill covering particular consignments, has been negotiated and that the proceeds received in accordance with exchange control regulations in the approved manner.

Documents Related To Inspection

Certificate of Inspection

It is a certificate issued by the Export Inspection Agency, certifying that the consignment has been inspected as required under the Export (Quality Control and Inspection) Ad, 1963, and satisfies the conditions relating to quality control and inspection as applicable to it, and is certified export worthy.

E. Documents Related to Excisable Goods

(i) G.P. Forms

A GP form is a gate pass for the removal of excisable goods from a factory or warehouse. Form GP 1 is used for the removal of excisable goods on payment of duty and form GP 2 is used for the removal of excisable goods without payment of duty.

(ii) Form C

Form C is to be used for applying for rebate of duty on the excisable goods (other than vegetable, non-essential oils and tea) exported by sea. It is to be submitted in triplicate to the Collector of Central Excises.

(iii) Forms A.R.-4/A.R.-4A

These forms are meant for applying for the removal of excisable goods for export by sea / post. Form A.R.-4 is used for applying for excise inspection at the factory and form A.R.-4A is used when goods are to be exported under a claim for rebate of excise duty or under bond.

F. Documents Related to Foreign Exchange Regulation

Foreign exchange regulations in India require the exporter to fill several forms. There are four important types of forms, namely, GR\PP, VP\COD and SOFTEX form for export of computer software obtainable from the RBI or a bank authorised to deal the foreign exchange.

Introduction

Export procedure describes the documents required for exporting from India. Special documents may be required depending on the type of product or destination. Certain export products may require a quality control inspection certificate from the Export Inspection Agency. Some food and pharmaceutical product may require a health or sanitary certificate for export. Export procedure consists of several commercial and regulatory formalities, which an exporter is required to complete during the course of export trade transaction. These formalities are very complex and time-consuming and involve considerable documentation. Hence, the exporters must possess adequate knowledge of such formalities. At the same time, it should be ensured that the rules and regulations of not only exporting country but also of importing country are duly complied with. Last but not least, it should be ensured that all the required documents, whether commercial or regulatory, are prepared and filed with the appropriate authorities. An export procedure can be studied under the following heads:

a) Registration Stage

b) Pre-shipment Stage

c) Shipment Stage

d) Post-Shipment Stage

Registration Stage

The exporter is required to register his organisation with a number of institutions and authorities, which directly or indirectly help him in the smooth conduct of export trade. The registration stage includes:

1. Registration of the Organisation

2. Opening Bank Account

3. Obtaining Import Export Code Number (IEC No)

4. Obtaining Permanent Account Number (PAN)

5. Obtaining Sales Tax Number

6. Registration with Export Promotion Council (EPC)

7. Registration with other Authorities

1) Registration of the Organisation

The form of organisation selected by the exporter must be registered under the appropriate Act of the country.

- A joint stock company under the companies act, 1956
- A partnership firm under the Indian Partnership Act, 1932
- A sole trader under local authorities

2) Opening Bank Account

The exporter should open a current account in the name of the firm or company with a commercial bank which is authorized by the Reserve Bank of India (RBI) to deal in foreign exchange. Such bank also serves as a source of pre-shipment and post-shipment finance for the exporter.

3) Obtaining Import Export Code Number (IEC No)

Prior to 1.1.1997, it was obligatory for every exporter to obtain CNX number from the RBI. However, since then, the CNX number has been replaced by IEC number issued by the Director General for Foreign Trade (DGFT).

4) Obtaining Permanent Account Number (PAN)

Export income is subject to a number of exemptions and deductions under different sections of the Income Tax Act. For claiming such exemptions and deductions, the exporter should register his organisation with the Income Tax Authorities and obtain the Permanent Account Number (PAN).

5) Obtaining Sales Tax Number

Exportable goods are exempted from sales tax, provided the exporter or his firm is registered with the Sales Tax Authorities. For this purpose, the exporter is required to make an application in the prescribed form to the Sales Tax Office (STO) in whose jurisdiction his (exporter's) office is situated.

6) Registration with Export Promotion Council (EPC)

It is obligatory for every exporter to register with the appropriate Export Promotion Council (EPC) and obtain the 'Registration- cum-Membership Certificate' (RCMC). The benefits provided in the current EXIM Policy are extended only to the registered exporters having valid RCMC. Registration with ECGC The exporter should also register with the Export Credit and Guarantee Corporation of India (ECGC) in order to secure overseas payments against political and commercial risks. It also helps the exporters in obtaining the financial assistance from commercial banks and other financial institutions.

7) Registration with other Authorities

The exporter should also register with various other authorities, such as:

- Federation of Indian Export Organisation (FIEO)
- Indian Trade Promotion Organisation (ITPO)
- Chambers of Commerce (COC)
- Productivity Councils, etc

Pre-Shipment Stage

Pre-shipment Stage Consists of the Following Steps

1) Approaching Foreign Buyers

In order to secure an export order, a new exporter can make use of one or more of the techniques, such as, advertising in international media, sales promotion, public relation, personal selling, publicity and participation in trade fairs and exhibitions.

2) Inquiry and Offer

An inquiry is a request from a prospective importer about description of goods, their standard or grade, size, weight or quantity, terms of payments, etc. On getting an inquiry, the exporter must process it immediately by making an offer in the form of a Proforma invoice.

3) Confirmation of Order

Once the negotiations are completed and the terms and conditions are finalised, the exporter sends three copies of Proforma invoice to the importer for the confirmation of order. The importer signs these copies and sends back two copies to the exporter.

4) Opening Letter of Credit

The documentary credit or letter of credit is the most appropriate and secured method of payment adopted to settle international transactions. On finalisation of the export contract, the importer opens a letter of credit in favour of the exporter, if agreed upon in the contract.

5) Arrangement of Pre-shipment Finance

On securing the letter of credit, the exporter procures a pre-shipment finance from his bank for procuring raw materials and other components, processing and packing of goods and transfer of goods to the port of shipment.

6) Production or Procurement of Goods

On securing the preshipment finance from the bank, the exporter either arranges for the production of the required goods or procures them from the domestic market as per the specifications of the importer.

7) Packing and Marking

Then the goods should be properly packed and marked with necessary details such as port of shipment and destination, country of origin, gross and net weight, etc. It required, assistance can be taken from the Indian Institute of Packing (IIP).

8) Pre-Shipment Inspection

If the goods to be exported are subject to compulsory quality control and pre-shipment inspection then the exporter should contact the Export inspection Agency (E!A) for obtaining an inspection certificate.

9) Central Excise Clearance

The exporters are totally exempted from the payment of central excise duty. However, the exemption should be claimed in one of the following ways namely Export under Rebate and Export under Bond.

10) Obtaining Insurance Cover

The exporter must take appropriate ECCE policy in order to cover credit risks policies and Marine policy, if the price quotation agreed upon is CIF.

11) Appointment of C&F Agent

Since exporting is a complex and time-consuming process, the exporter should appoint a Clearing and Forwarding (C&F) agent for the smooth clearance of goods from the customs and preparation and submission of various export documents.

Shipment Stage

Export cargo can be exported to the overseas buyer by sea, air or land. However, shipment by sea is the most popular and generally resorted to, as it is comparatively cheaper. Besides, the ship's capacity is far greater than other modes of transportation. Nevertheless, transportation by air is utilised for export of expensive items like, diamonds, gold, etc. The shipment stage includes the following steps:

1) Reservation of Shipping Space

Once the export contract is finalised, the exporter reserves the required space in the vessel for shipment. On accepting the exporter's request, the shipping company issues a Shipping Order. The original copy of the shipping order is given to the exporter and the duplicate is sent to the commanding officer of the ship. The shipping order is an instruction by the shipping company to the commanding officer of the ship that the goods as per the details given should be received on board.

2) Arrangement of Internal Transportation up to the Port of Shipment

The exporter makes necessary arrangements for transportation of goods to the port either by road or railways. On loading goods into the railway wagon, the railway authorities issue a 'Railway Receipt', which may be either 'freight paid' o 'freight to pay'. It serves as a title to the goods. The export endorses the railway receipt in favour of his agent to enable him to take delivery of the goods at the port of shipment.

3) Preparation and Processing

As the goods reach the port of shipment, the exporter should issue detailed instructions to the C&F agent for the shipment of cargo along with a complete set of the documents listed below

- Letter of Credit along with the export contract or export order
- Commercial Invoice
- Packing List or Packing Note
- Certificate of Origin
- GR Form (original and duplicate)
- ARE-I Form.
- Certificate of Inspection, where necessary (original copy)
- Marine Insurance Policy

4) Customs Clearance

The cargo must be cleared from the Customs before it is loaded on the ship. For this, the above mentioned documents, along with five copies of shipping bill, are to be submitted to the Customs Appraiser at the Customs House. The Customs Appraiser ensures that all the formalities relating to exchange control, quality control, pre- shipment inspection and licensing have been complied with by the exporter. After verification, | all documents, except the original GR, original copy of Shipping Bill and one copy of Commercial Invoice, are returned to the C&F agent.

5) Obtaining 'Carting Order' from the Port Trust Authorities

The C&F agent, then, approaches the Superintendent of the concerned Port Trust for obtaining the 'Carting Order' for moving the cargo inside the dock. After obtaining the Carting Order, the cargo is physically moved into the port area and stored in the appropriate shed.

6) Customs Examination and Issue of 'Let Export Order'

Custom Examiner at the port shipment physically examines the goods and seals the packages in his presence. The same can be arranged for at the factory or warehouse of the exporter by making an application to the Assistant Collector of Customs. The Customs Examiner, if satisfied, issues a formal permission for the loading of cargo on the ship in the form of a 'Let Export Order'.

7) Obtaining 'Let Ship Order' from the Customs Preventive Officer

'Let Export Order' must be supplemented by a 'Let Ship Order' issued by the Customs Preventive Officer. The C&F agent submits the duplicate copy of Shipping Bill, duly endorsed by the Customs Examiner, to the Customs Preventive Officer who endorses it with the 'Let Ship Order'.

8) Obtaining Mate's Receipt and Bill of Lading

The goods are then loaded on board the ship for which the Mate or the Captain of the ship issues Mate's Receipt to the Port Superintendent. The Port Superintendent, on receipt of port dues, hands over the Mate's Receipt to the C&F Agent. The C&F Agent surrenders the Mate's Receipt to the Shipping Company for obtaining the Bill of Lading. The Shipping Company issues two to three negotiable and two to three non-negotiable copies of Bill of Lading.

Post-Shipment Stage

1) Submission of Documents by the C&F Agent to the Exporter

On the completion of the shipping procedure, the C&F agent submits the following documents to the exporter:

- A copy of invoice duly attested by the Customs
- Drawback copy of the shipping bill
- Export promotion copy of the shipping bill
- A full set of negotiable and non-negotiable copies of bill of lading
- The original L/C, export order or contract.
- Duplicate copy of the ARE-I form.

2) Shipment Advice to Importer

After the shipment of goods, the exporter intimates the importer about the shipment of goods giving him details about the date of shipment, the name of the vessel, the destination, etc. He should also send one copy of non-negotiable bill of lading to the importer.

3) Presentation of Documents to Bank for Negotiation

Submission of relevant documents to the bank and the process of getting the payment from the bank are called "Negotiation of the Documents" and the documents are called 'Negotiable Set of Documents'. The set normally contains

- Bill of Exchange, Sight Draft or Usance Draft
- Full set of Bill of Lading or Airway Bill
- Original Letter of Credit
- Customs Invoice
- Commercial Invoice
- Packing List
- Foreign exchange declaration forms
- Exchange control copy of the Shipping Bill
- Certificate of Origin, GSP or APR Certificate, etc
- Marine Insurance Policy

4) Dispatch of Documents

The bank negotiates these documents to the importer's bank in the manner as specified in the L/C. Before negotiating documents, the exporter's bank scrutinises them in order to ensure that all formalities have been complied with and all documents are in order. The bank then sends the Bank Certificate and attested copies of commercial invoice to the exporter.

5) Acceptance of the Bill of Exchange

Bill of exchange accompanied by the above documents is known as the Documentary Bill of Exchange. It is of two types

Documents against Payment (Sight Drafts)

In case of sight draft,the drawer instructs the bank to hand over the relevant documents to the importer only against payment.

Documents against Acceptance (Usance Draft)

In case of usance draft, the drawer instructs the bank to hand over the relevant documents to the importer against his 'acceptance' of the bill of exchange.

6) Letter of Indemnity

The exporter can get immediate payment from his bank on the submission of documents by signing a letter of indemnity. By signing the letter of indemnity the exporter undertakes to indemnify the bank in the event of non-receipt of payment from the importer along with accrued interests.

7)Realisation of Export Proceeds

On receiving the documentary bill of exchange, the importer releases payment in case of sight draft or accepts the usance draft undertaking to pay on maturity of the bill of exchange. The exporter's bank receives the payment through importer's bank and is credited to exporter's account.

8)Processing of GR Form

On receiving the export proceeds, 'the exporter's bank intimates the same to the RBI by recording the fact on the duplicate copy of GR. The RBI verifies the details in duplicate copy of GR with the original copy of GR received from the Customs. If the details are found to be in order then the export transaction is treated to be completed.

9)Realisation of Export Incentives

If the exporter is eligible for export incentives, then he should submit claim for the same accompanied by the bank certificate to the appropriate authority.

EXIM BANK

The Export-Import (EXIM) Bank of India is the principal financial institution in India for coordinating the working of institutions engaged in financing export and import trade. It is a statutory corporation wholly owned by the Government of India. It was established on January 1, 1982 for the purpose of financing, facilitating and promoting foreign trade of India. Government of India launched the institution with a mandate to not just enhance exports from India, but also to integrate the country's foreign trade and investment with the overall economic growth. Exim Bank of India has been both a catalyst and a key player in the promotion of cross border trade and investment. Commencing operations as a purveyor of export credit, like other Export Credit Agencies in the world, Exim Bank of India has evolved into an institution that plays a major role in partnering Indian industries, particularly the Small and Medium Enterprises through a wide range of products and services offered at all stages of the business cycle, starting from import of technology and export product development to export production, export marketing, pre- shipment and post-shipment and overseas investment.

The authorised capital of the EXIM Bank is Rs. 200 crores and paid up capital is Rs. 100 crores, wholly subscribed by the Central Government. The bank can raise additional resources through:

1. Loans/grants from Central Government and Reserve Bank of India;
2. Lines of credit from institutions abroad;
2. Funds raised from Euro Currency markets;
3. Bonds issued in India.

Main Objectives of EXIM Bank

1. To ensure and integrated and coordinated approach in solving the allied problems encountered by exporters in India.
2. To pay specific attention to the exports of capital goods;
3. Export projection;
4. To facilitate and encourage joint ventures and export of technical services and international and merchant banking;
5. To extend buyers' credit and lines of credit;
6. To tap domestic and foreign markets for resources for undertaking development and financial activities in the export sector.

Functions of Foreign Exchange Department

The foreign exchange department is a highly specialised department in a bank. A wide variety of services are rendered by a foreign exchange department. Broadly, the functions of a foreign exchange department may be classified as:

1. Financing exports,
2. Financing imports,
3. Remittance facilities
4. Providing remittance facilities,
5. Dealing in foreign exchange, and
6. Furnishing credit information.

1. Financing Exports

The financial needs of the exporter right from the moment he conceives of the project and till he realises export proceeds are provided by banks. The credit extended to the exporter to procure raw materials, process them and prepare them for shipment to the importer is known as packing credit or pre-shipment credit On shipping the goods the exporter would draw a bill of exchange, with or without a letter of credit and discount it with the bank. The credit extended to the exporter after shipment is made is known as post-shipment finance. The exporter may be eligible to receive cash incentives from the Govern- ment on exports. Finance may be made available to the bank again such entitlements. This may cover both pre-shipment and post-shipment stages. The advances to exporters, export being a preferred sector, are made at a concessional rate of interest. Banks get refinance on eligible advances.

Besides financing, the other service rendered by banks to exporters is advising/confirming letters, of credit drawn in favor of the exporters by their correspondents abroad. Even if the exporter does not require any financial accommodation from the bank, the exchange control regulations require him to receive the export proceeds only through an authorised dealer. Therefore, the export bills are to be collected through a bank. The bank may also execute guarantees on behalf of its export customers.

2. Financing Imports

Letters of credit are issued by banks on behalf of their importer-customers. The opening of the letter of credit by the bank, whereby, it undertakes to make payment to the exporter on shipment, enables the importer to conclude the deal with ease. The importer may be financed by the bank for the imports. This finance may take any form, cash credit or loan, as the case may be, and against hypothecation or pledge or mortgage of the item imported. The, exporter abroad is paid by the bank in foreign exchange. The bank may issue deferred payment guarantees on behalf of the importer for items purchased on terms of payment of price on a long-term basis. The import of goods into India is subject to the Import Trade Policy of the Government and exchange control regulations of the Reserve Bank. The Bank takes care to see that they are adhered to.

3. Remittance Facilities

An importer in India has to pay the overseas exporter. Similarly, an Indian exporter has to receive payment from abroad. A person in India may like to subscribe to a magazine published abroad. An Indian who is now employed abroad may like to remit funds for maintenance of his family in India. The payments into or from India can be arranged through any of the credit instruments. Briefly, the instruments may be described thus:

(a) Telegraphic Transfer

It is an instruction sent by the bank by telegram (i.e., by cable) to its branch at a foreign centre or to its correspondent bank abroad to pay a certain sum to the person named therein. This is the quickest means of remittance and the beneficiary can obtain payment the very next day of remittance.

(b) Mail Transfer

This is similar to a telegraphic transfer with a difference that instead of the order being sent by cable it is sent through mail. As can be expected, there would be some delay, say, about a week or ten days, before the beneficiary can obtain payment.

(c) Bank Draft or Demand Draft

It is an order to pay a certain sum to a certain person or his order issued by the bank on its overseas branch or on its correspondent bank. The demand draft is handed over to the purchaser who sends it to the beneficiary. The beneficiary obtains payment on presentation to the bank on which the draft is drawn.

(d) Foreign Traveller's Cheques

For the convenience of tourists, banks issue travelers cheques in major currencies of the world. They can be encased at any bank in majority of countries. The traveler signs at one place in the travelers' cheque while purchasing it. He is required to sign again on the travelers' cheque before encashing bank. The encashing bank gets reimbursement by sending it to the issuing bank.

(e) Bill of Exchange

The exporter may draw a bill on the importer covering the export and sell the bill to the bank. The purchasing bank would send the bill to its overseas branch or its correspondent bank who would present it to the person on whom it is drawn. The purchasing bank's account would be credited on realisation of the bill. For the benefit of Indians residing abroad, banks open and maintain nonresident accounts.

4. Dealing in Foreign Exchange

Banks buy and sell foreign exchange from and to the public. To carry out this function banks have to keep sufficient stock of foreign exchange. These are kept in the form of bank accounts abroad. Banks maintain accounts with banks in important financial centres abroad through which all sales and purchases of foreign exchange are routed. For example, a foreign demand draft in pound-sterling issued by the bank would be made payable by the bank in London with which it maintains an account. On presentation of the draft in London, the bank's account would be debited. Bank's dealing in foreign exchange may sometimes necessitate it to sell to or buy from other banks in the place, or the Reserve Bank, the required foreign currency.

5. Furnishing Credit Information

With a network of correspondent relationships with banks abroad, a bank in India is in a position to furnish business information to exporters and importers in India. The information may relate to the credit report on the prospective seller/buyer, market conditions, exchange control regulations in different countries, etc. The bank is also in a position to advise the customer of such other matter as the currency in which the transaction is to be designated and avoidance of exchange risk. Thus the foreign exchange department of a bank renders many useful services to exporters and importers. The bank should keep itself constantly updated and be in touch with the latest trend in international markets.

Financial Products of Exim Bank

1. Overseas Investment Finance Programme

Exim Bank encourages Indian companies to invest abroad for, inter alias, setting up manufacturing units and for acquiring overseas companies to get access to the foreign market, technology, raw material, brand, IPR etc. For financing such overseas investments, Exim Bank provides:

a.   Term loans to Indian companies up to 80% of their equity investment in overseas Joint ventures.

b. Term loans to Indian companies towards up to 80% of loan extended by them to the overseas Joint ventures.

c. Term loans to overseas Joint ventures towards part financing

- capital expenditure towards acquisition of assets
- working capital
- equity investment in another company
- acquisition of brands/ patents/ rights/ other IPR
- acquisition of another company

d. Guarantee facility to the overseas joint ventures

2. Project Exports

Project exports occupy an important place in India's export portfolio. The contracts secured in the recent years have been quite diverse in nature, indicating the growing versatility and technological capabilities of Indian project exporters. Projects involve activities like engineering, procurement, construction including provision of all desired and specified equipment and / supplies, construction and building materials, consultancy, technical know-how, technology transfer, design, engineering , commissioning with other all such related services as are needed by the existing or new projects / plants / processes involving international competitive bidding (thus including even Multilaterally Funded Projects in India). Exim Bank extends funded and non-funded facilities for overseas turnkey projects, civil construction contracts, technical and consultancy service contracts as well as supplies.

Turnkey Projects are those which involve supply of equipment along with related services, like design, detailed engineering, civil construction, erection and commissioning of plants and power transmission & distribution

Construction Projects involve civil works, steel structural works, as well as associated supply of construction material and equipment for various infrastructure projects.

Technical and Consultancy Service contracts, involving provision of know-how, skills, personnel and training are categorised as consultancy projects. Typical examples of services contracts are: project implementation services, management contracts, and super vision of erection of plants, CAD / CAM solutions in software exports, finance and accounting systems.

Supplies: Supply contracts involve primarily export of capital goods and industrial manufactures. Typical examples of supply contracts are: supply of stainless steel slabs and Ferro-chrome manufacturing equipments, diesel generators, pumps and compressors.

3. Line of Credit

A Line of Credit (LOC) is a financing mechanism through which Exim Bank extends support for export of projects, equipment, goods and services from India. Exim Bank extends Line of credit on its own and also at the behest and with the support of Government of India. Exim Bank extends Lines of Credit to:

a. Foreign Governments or their nominated agencies such as central banks, state owned commercial banks
b. National or regional development banks
c. Overseas financial institutions
d. Commercial banks abroad
e. Other suitable overseas entities

The above mentioned recipients of Line of credit act as intermediaries and on lend to overseas buyers for import of Indian equipment, goods and services. LOC is a financing mechanism that provides a safe mode of non-recourse financing option to Indian exporters to enter new export markets or expand business in existing export markets without any payment risk from the overseas importers.

4. Corporate Banking

The Bank offers a number of financing programmes for Export Oriented Units (EOUs), importers and for companies making overseas investments. The financing programmes cater to the term loan requirements of Indian exporters for financing their new project, expansion, modernization, purchase of equipment, R&D, overseas investments and also the working capital requirements.

a. Research & Development Finance for Export Oriented Units

Exim Bank encourages Indian exporters to invest more in their R&D spending in order to develop new products/processes for enhancing export capabilities. Considering the need to bridge the funding gap of Indian exporters in R&D space, the Bank has a dedicated R&D Financing Programme. Under the said Programme, financing for R&D can be extended to any export oriented company. The financing covers both capital and revenue expenditure. They are

1. Land and building, civil works for housing eligible R&D activities;
2. Equipments, tools, computer hardware/ software, miscellaneous fixed assets used in eligible R&D activities;

3. Acquisition of technology from India or overseas at the "proof of concept" or design stage, which will be used to develop new product/ process.

4. Salaries of R&D personnel, support staff during the R&D project phase including training costs;

5. Cost of regulatory approvals, filing and maintenance of patent registration;

6. Product documentation and allied costs during the R&D project phase.

7. Costs of materials, surveys, technology demonstration studies and field trial

b. Pre-shipment/Post-shipment Credit Programme

Exim Bank extends export credit to Indian exporters to meet a wide range of trade financing requirements for execution of an export transaction. The Bank provides working capital finance by way pre-shipment credit and post-shipment credit. Bank also extends as part of export credit assistance, non-fund based limits inter alia including issuance of Letters of Credit (both Foreign & inland) and Bank Guarantees (both Foreign & inland) for its clients. The credit limits are generally extended as part of Borrower's consortium limit and are operated as a running account facility. The limits may be renewed for further period subject to satisfactory review of account and depending on the Borrower's export credit requirement. The facilities can be drawn in either Indian Rupee or Foreign Currency.

c. Lending Programme for Export Oriented Units

Exim Bank provides term loans to export oriented Indian companies to finance various capital expenditures including certain soft expenditures in order to improve their export capability and to enhance their international competitiveness. Loans/Guarantees are extended for the following purposes: Expansion, modernization, up gradation or diversification projects including acquisition of equipment, technology etc.; export marketing; export product development; setting up of Software Technology Parks;

d. SME-ADB line

Exim Bank has arranged for a credit line from the Asian Development Bank (ADB) for providing foreign currency term loans to the Micro, Small and Medium Enterprises borrowers in certain specific lagging states of India, viz. Assam, Madhya Pradesh, Odissa, Uttar Pradesh, Chhattisgarh, Jharkhand,

Rajasthan and Uttarakhand. These foreign currency term loans can also finance domestic capital expenditure of the borrowers in Indian Rupees, besides meeting their foreign currency capital expenditure requirements. The assistance to these Micro, Small and Medium Enterprises will help in increasing competitiveness in the relatively backward states and help in integrating them into the mainstream economy.

e. Technology & Innovation Enhancement and Infrastructure Development Fund

With a view to facilitate credit flow to the Micro, Small and Medium Enterprises sector at competitive rates, Exim Bank has set up a Technology and Innovation Enhancement and Infrastructure Development (TIEID) fund of USD 500 mn exclusively for Micro, Small and Medium Enterprises , to augment their export competitiveness and internationalisation efforts, by partnering with banks. TIEID seeks to meet long term foreign currency loan requirements of Indian exporting entities in the Micro, Small and Medium Enterprises sector for meeting capital expenditure, through refinancing of Banks against their eligible Micro, Small and Medium Enterprises financing portfolio.

f. Lending Programme for Financing Creative Economy

The Creative Industries are those industries which have their origin in individual creativity, skill and talent and which have a potential for wealth and Job creation through the generation and exploitation of intellectual property viz., Advertising, Architecture, Art and Antiques Market, Crafts,Design, Designer Fashion, Film and Video, Interactive Leisure Software, Music, Performing Arts, Publishing, Software and Computer Services, Television and Radio etc. In view of the large untapped potential for increasing exports by the creative industries and in order to provide a strategic focus to this sector and enhance Exim Bank's presence in the creative economy space, and as a corollary, in the MSME segment, Exim Bank has introduced a Programme specifically for financing the Creative Economy.

g. Finance for Gross Root Enterprises

The Bank supports globalisation of enterprises based out of rural areas of the country through its GRID programme. Through this initiative, the Bank extends financial support to promote grassroots initiatives/technologies, particularly those having export potential. The objective of the programme is to help artisans/producer groups/clusters/small enterprises across the country realize remunerative return on their produce essentially through facilitating exports from these units. The group handles credit proposals from such organizations working at the rural /grassroots level and offers tailor-made financial products to cater to their needs. The group is mandated to work towards developing a robust, vibrant and holistic approach in its intervention by providing assistance at various stages of product development / business cycle including capacity building, export capability creation, expansion/diversification and finally exports. The broad areas of support extended by the Bank through its grassroots initiatives inter alia, include capacity building, development of common facility centres, construction of raw material bank, technology up gradation and creation of export capability.

5. Buyer's Credit

Overseas buyers/importers can avail this facility for import of eligible goods and services from India on deferred payment terms. The facility enables exporters/contractors to expand abroad and into non- traditional markets. It also enables exporters/contractors to be competitive when bidding or negotiating for overseas jobs. Buyer's Credit is extended to a foreign project company that intends to award the project execution to an Indian project exporter. The financing will be available to all kinds of projects and service exports from India.

Facility is available for development, upgrading or expansion of infrastructure facilities; financing of public or private projects such a plants and buildings; professional services such as surveyors, architecture, consultations, etc. It enables overseas buyers to obtain medium-and long-term financing and providing competitive interest rate against host country's high cost of borrowing;

Services of Exim Bank

1. Research & Analysis

Exim Bank's Research & Analysis Group (RAG) offers a vast range of research products. The Bank's team of experienced economists and strategists provide insights on aspects of international economics, trade and investment through qualitative and quantitative research techniques. RAG monitors the global trends in the world and domestic economies and the impact of these trends, especially on India and other developing economies. RAG caters to the constituents within the Bank, as well as to those external to the Bank such as Government, RBI, exporters/importers, trade & industry associations, external credit agencies, academic institutions and researchers. The research work carried out in the Group under the broad classification of regional, Sectoral and policy related studies are published in the form of Occasional Papers, Working Papers, Books, etc. These research studies primarily envisage identifying avenues for enhancing India's international engagement.

The group also undertakes country profiles, which assess the economic, political, currency and credit risks involved, along with the export opportunities in the country concerned. Further the profiles provide short-to-medium term economic outlook of a country, indicating the economic risk involved in doing business with country. Further, the group also prepares exposure limit for countries of business interest to the Bank, and similarly tracks development in the key industries for the benefit of the Bank's business exposure in these industries.

2. Marketing Advisory Services

Exim Bank plays a promotional role and seeks to create and enhance export capabilities and international competitiveness of Indian companies. Exim Bank through its Marketing Advisory Services helps Indian exporting firms in their globalisation efforts by proactively assisting in locating overseas distributor(s)/ buyer(s)/ partner(s) for their products and services. The Bank assists in identification of opportunities overseas for setting up plants or projects or for acquisition of companies overseas. MAS Group leverages the Bank's high international standing, in-depth knowledge and understanding of the international markets and well established institutional linkages, coupled with its physical presence, to support Indian companies in their overseas marketing initiatives on a success fee basis. The fees for Marketing Advisory Service is payable in Indian Rupees and applies to the subsequent orders from the client introduced by the Bank for a period of at least 2 years.

Exim Bank has been able to successfully place a range of products in overseas as well as domestic market. The products list includes Handmade Paper, Handicrafts, Vegetables and Fresh Fruits, Garments, Home Décor, Marine Products, Spices and Agri Equipments etc which were placed in Singapore, Africa, Brazil, Middle East, and US. MAS Group also organizes workshops and supporting events for facilitating to design and package their products for the international markets.

3. Export Advisory Services Group

The Export Advisory Services Group offers a diverse range of information, advisory and support services, which enable exporters to evaluate international risks, exploit export opportunities and improve competitiveness. Value added information and support services are provided to Indian projects exporters on the projects funded by multilateral agencies. The Group undertakes customised research on behalf of interested companies in the areas such as establishing market potential, defining marketing arrangements, and specifying market distribution channels. Developing export market entry plans, facilitating accomplishment of international quality certification and display of products in trade fairs and exhibitions are other services provided.

The Bank provides a wide range of information, advisory and support services, which complement its financing programmes. These services are provided on a fee basis to Indian companies and overseas entities. The scope of services includes market-related information, sector and feasibility studies, technology supplier identification, partner search, investment facilitation and development of joint ventures both in India and abroad. During the year, the Bank provided a range of services to companies. Information in the form of a list of importers / exporters across different industries and sectors was provided to Indian firms active in international trade

a. Multilateral Funded Projects Overseas

The Bank provides a package of information and support services to Indian companies to help improve their prospects for securing business in projects funded by the World Bank, Asian Development Bank, African Development Bank, and European Bank for Reconstruction and Development. During the year, the Bank disseminated information on numerous overseas business opportunities to various Indian companies covering various sectors including transportation, construction, telecommunication, energy, infrastructure, educational and information technology.

b. Exim Bank as a Consultant

The Bank's experience in evolving as an institution supporting international trade and investment, in addition to functioning as an export credit agency in a developing country context, is of particular relevance in other developing countries. The Bank has been sharing its experience and expertise by undertaking consultancy assignments. Exim Bank also shares its experience and expertise through provision of on-site exchange of personnel programmes aimed at providing a first-hands experience to the employees of its institutional partners.

c. Institutional Linkages

The Bank has fostered a network of alliances and institutional linkages with multilateral agencies, export credit agencies, banks and financial institutions, trade promotion bodies, and investment promotion boards to help create an enabling environment for supporting trade and investment.

d. Global Network of Exim Banks and Development Financial Institutions

The Global Network of Exim Banks and Development Finance Institutions (G-NEXID) was set up in Geneva in March 2006 through the Bank's initiative, under the auspices of UNCTAD. With the active support of a number of other Exim Banks and Development Finance Institutions from various developing countries, the network has endeavored to foster enhanced South-South trade and investment cooperation, characterized among others.

e. Award for Excellence

The Bank, in association with CII, has instituted an Annual Award for Business Excellence for best Total Quality Management (TQM) practices adopted by an Indian company. The Award is based on the European Foundation for Quality Management (EFQM) model.

EXPORT CREDIT AND GUARANTEE CORPORATION

Introduction

ECGC is essentially an export promotion organization, seeking to improve the competitive capacity of Indian exporters by giving them credit insurance covers comparable to those available to their competitors from most other countries. It keeps it's premium rates at the lowest level possible. Export Credit Guarantee Corporation of India Ltd. (ECGC) is a Government of India Enterprise which provides export credit insurance facilities to exporters and banks in India. It functions under the administrative control of Ministry of Commerce & Industry, and is managed by a Board of Directors comprising representatives of the Government, Reserve Bank of India, banking, and insurance and exporting community. Over the years, it has evolved various export credit risk insurance products to suit the requirements of Indian exporters and commercial banks. ECGC is the seventh largest credit insurer of the world in terms of coverage of national exports. The present paid up capital of the Company is Rs. 1200 Crores and the authorized capital is Rs. 5000 Crores. It provides a range of credit risk insurance covers to exporters against loss in export of goods and services. It offers Export Credit Insurance covers to banks and financial institutions to enable exporters to obtain better facilities from them. It also provides Overseas Investment Insurance to Indian companies investing in joint ventures abroad in the form of equity or loan

The company considers itself as a trustee of its stakeholders and acknowledges its responsibility towards them for creation and safeguarding stakeholders' wealth and interests. During the year under review, the company continued its pursuit of achieving these objectives through adoption and monitoring of corporate strategies, prudent business plans, monitoring of major risks of the Corporation's business and pursuing policies and procedures to satisfy legal and ethical responsibilities.

Background of ECGC

The need for export promotion had started immediately after Independence in 1947. In 1953, a proposal for initiation of an export credit guarantee scheme was put forward at a meeting of the Export Advisory Council. Ministry of Commerce & Industry analyzed in depth the pros and cons of the Export Credit Insurance Scheme and a revised draft proposal on the scheme were presented to the Export Advisory Council in 1955. Shri T T Krishnamachari, Finance Minister in Nehru's cabinet appointed a special committee under the Chairmanship of Shri T.C.Kapur to examine the feasibility of setting up an effective organization to provide insurance against export credit risks. The Government accepted the recommendations of Kapur Committee and thus the Export Risk Insurance Corporation (ERIC) was registered on 30th July 1957 in Mumbai as a Private Ltd. Company, entirely state owned, under the Companies Act with an authorized capital of Rs.5 crores and paid up capital of Rs.25 lakhs. Shri Ratilal M Gandhi was the First Chairman and Shri T C Kapur was the First Managing Director of the Corporation. Shri Morarji Desai, Union Commerce Minister inaugurated ERIC and the first Policy was issued on 14th October 1957. After introduction of insurance covers to banks during the period 1962-64, ERIC's name was changed to Export Credit & Guarantee Corporation Ltd in 1964. To bring Indian identify in the name, ECGC was renamed as Export Credit Guarantee Corporation of India Ltd in the year 1983.

Objectives of ECGC

The Corporation has set before itself the following objectives:

1. To offer insurance protection to exporters against payment risks
2. To provide guidance in export-related activities
3. To make available information on different countries with it's own credit ratings
4. To make it easy to obtain export finance from banks/financial institutions
5. To assist exporters in recovering bad debts
6. To provides information on credit-worthiness of overseas buyers
7. To encourage and facilitate globalization of India's trade.
8. To assist Indian exporters in managing their credit risks by providing timely information on worthiness of the buyers, bankers and the countries
9. To facilitate availability of adequate bank finance to the Indian exporters by providing surety insurance covers for bankers at competitive rates.
10. To achieve improved performance in terms of profitability, financial and operational efficiency indicators and achieve optimum return on investment.
11. To develop world class expertise in credit insurance among employees and ensure continuous innovation and achieve the highest customer satisfaction by delivering top quality
12. To protect the Indian exporters against unforeseen losses, which may arise due to failure of the buyer, bank or problems faced by the country of the buyer by providing cost effective credit insurance covers in the form of Policy, Factoring and Investment Insurance Services comparable to similar covers available to exporters in other countries.

The National Export Insurance Account

The National Export Insurance Account has been set up by the Government of India and operated by ECGC to provide adequate credit insurance cover to protect long and medium term exporters against both, political and commercial risks of the overseas country and the buyer/bank concerned. The NEIA trust also provides covers to banks for Buyer's Credit transactions which facilitates foreign buyer to pay for project exports from India. Indian companies secure overseas projects against stiff international competition and needs adequate credit insurance to enhance their competitiveness. Projects are required to be undertaken, specifically due to the long term economic interest and political relationship of India with importing country. Given India's long term economic and political interests with the concerned country, it is crucial that ability of Indian exporters undertaking such contracts is not hampered by the inability to obtain credit insurance cover. With this view Government of India has set up the NEIA.

ECGC, apart from insuring credit risks under short term exports also provides credit insurance cover to Medium and Long term exporters. However, at times, its own limitations make it difficult for ECGC to cover such risks on purely commercial considerations, taking into account the long repayment period, the large value of the contracts and the difficult economic and political conditions of the country, coupled with the fact that reinsurance cover is generally not available in such cases. The NEIA is a public trust set up by the Government will manage the funds provided by the Government. The trust has been assured a corpus of Rs.2,000 crores by the end of the 11th plan period. At any point of time an exposure equal to ten times of the corpus will be underwritten by NEIA subject other criteria.

Risks in International Trade

Payments for exports are open to risks even at the best of times. The risks have assumed large proportions today due to the far-reaching political and economic changes that are sweeping the world. An outbreak of war or civil war may block or delay payment for goods exported. A coup or an insurrection may also bring about the same result. Economic difficulties or balance of payment problems may lead a country to impose restrictions on either import of certain goods or on transfer of payments for goods imported. In addition, the exporters have to face commercial risks of insolvency or protracted default of buyers. The commercial risks of a foreign buyer going bankrupt or losing his capacity to pay are aggravated due to the political and economic uncertainties. Export credit insurance is designed to protect exporters from the consequences of the payment risks, both political and commercial, and to enable them to expand their overseas business without fear of loss.

Risks in foreign trade are the major barriers for the growth to the same. International trade has been a much debated topic. International trade can develop an economy, but at the same time certain domestic players can be outperformed by financially stronger multi nationals and forced to close down or get merged. Sometimes these multinational companies become so powerful, especially in smaller countries, that they can dictate political terms to the government for their benefit. The assessment of risks in the foreign trade plays an important role. The different risks involved in foreign trade has been explained as under

Economic Risks

- Risk of concession in economic control
- Risk of insolvency of the buyer
- Risk of non-acceptance
- Risk of protracted default
- Risk of Exchange rate

Political Risks

- Risk of non- renewal of import and exports licenses
- Risks due to war
- Risk of the imposition of an import ban after the delivery of the goods
- Surrendering of political sovereignty

Buyer Country Risks

- Changes in the policies of the government
- Exchange control regulations
- Lack of foreign currency
- Trade embargoes

Commercial Risk

- A bank's lack of ability to honor its responsibilities
- A buyer's failure pertaining to payment due to financial limitations
- A seller's inability to provide the required quantity or quality of goods

Others Risks

- Cultural differences
- Lack of knowledge of overseas markets
- Language barriers
- Inclination to corrupt business associates

- Legal protection for breach of contract or non-payment is low
- Effects of unpredictable business environment and fluctuating exchange rates
- Sovereign risk - the ability of the government of a country to pay off its debts
- Natural risk

Policies Issued by ECGC

Export Credit Guarantee Corporation of India is essentially an export promotion organization seeking to improve the competitive capacity of Indian exporters by giving them credit insurance. It provides wide range of insurance facilities to exporters, banks and financial institutions. One can study numerous insurance policies offered by Export Guarantee Corporation of India to comprehend the various policies offered by the company. Further, one can make comparison between various policies in order to select a policy covering every clause of their trade risk.

The insurance cover provided by Export Credit Guarantee Corporation of India also helps the exporters in getting better access to credit facilities from financial institutions. Export Credit Guarantee Corporation of India is the fifth largest credit insurance company which deals with exports of any country. Export Credit Guarantee Corporation of India provides a range of credit risk insurance covers to exporters against loss in export of goods and services and offers guarantees to banks and financial institutions to enable exporters to obtain better facilities from them. ECGC provides Overseas Investment Insurance to exporters and banks in the following ways.

I. Export Credit Insurance for Exporter
II. Export Credit Insurance for Banks
III. Export Credit Insurance Special Schemes

I. Export Credit Insurance for Exporter

1. Shipments Comprehensive Risks Policy

This policy is issued to exporters for a period of one year and whose turnover is more than 50 lakhs and is meant to cover risks is respect of goods exported on short term credit. This policy covers both commercial and political risks from the date of shipment.

2. Small Exporters Policy

This policy is meant for small exporters whose turnover is less than 50 lakhs and it is generally provided for one year. It also covers both commercial and political risks.

3. Specific Shipment Policy

This policy provide cover to the Indian exporters against commercial and political risks involved in export of goods on short term credit not exceeding 180 days. Exporters can take insurance either for a single shipment of for few shipments under the contract.

4. Services Policy

While serving contract for providing technical and professional services, payments under the contract are subject to risks and this policy provides cover to give a measure of protection to such exporters of services.

5. Export Turnover Policy

The turnover policy is issued for one year and the benefit of this policy is provided to large exporters who contribute more than RS 10 lakhs per annum towards premium. It provides cover to risks ranging from political to commercial risks.

6. Export Specific Buyer Policy

This policy provides cover to Indian exporters against commercial and political risks involved in export of goods on short term credit to a particular buyer.

7. Consignment Exports Policy

The consignment policy cover protects the Indian exporters from possible losses when selling goods to ultimate buyers. There are two policies available for covering consignment exports such as stock holding agent policy and global entity policy.

8. Buyer Exposure Policy

This policy is meant to provide exposure based cover on a selected buyer. The cover is available to provide commercial and political risks to the buyer for both LC and non-LC transactions. A separate buyer exposure policy is issued to each buyer covering all the exports to be made to the buyer during a period of twelve months.

9. IT-enabled Services Policy

This policy is issued to cover various commercial and political risks involved in rendering IT enabled services to a particular customer. The various commercial risks include insolvency of the customer, failure of the customer to make the payment within a specified period.

10. Small and Medium Enterprise Policy

This is a policy exclusively meant for small and medium enterprise sector units. It protects policy holders from various commercial risks such as insolvency of the buyer and insolvency of the LC opening bank.

11. Software Project Policy

This policy is specially meant for software exporters of the country namely software projects policy where payments will be received in foreign exchange. It includes various turnkey projects on progressive and milestone basis onsite and off-site locations of the companies.

12. Construction Works Policy

This policy is designed to provide cover to an Indian contractor who executes a civil construction job abroad. The policy is meant to protect the contractor from various risks such as insolvency of the employer and failure of the employer to pay the amounts that become payable to the contractor as per terms of the contract.

13. Specific Policy for Supply Contract

This policy is meant to provide a continuing insurance for the regular flow of an exporter's shipment for which credit period does not exceed 180 days. Contract of supply of capital goods or turnkey projects or rendering services abroad that are not of repetitive nature are insured by Export credit Guarantee Corporation on a case to case basis under specific contract plans.

14. Specific Shipment Policy

This policy is meant to provide protection against non-receipt of payments due to commercial or political risks. This policy can be obtained by exporters that have secured contract for supply of capital goods such as machinery or equipment on deferred terms of payment.

15. Specific Services Policy

This policy provides cover to protect payments for professional or technical services, hiring or leasing services can also be covered under the policy as payments are open to risk after expiration of supply contracts.

16. Letter of Confirmation Cover

When a bank in India adds its confirmation to a foreign letter of credit, it binds itself to honor the drafts drawn by the beneficiary of letter of credit without any recourse but in certain cases, banks will suffer loss if the foreign bank fails to reimburse it with the amount paid to the exporter.

Export Credit Insurance for Banks

1) Individual Packing Credit Insurance Policy

This policy provides protection to the banks against the losses that may be incurred in extending packing credit advances due to protracted default or insolvency of the exporter client. A bank or a financial institution authorized to deal in foreign exchange can obtain the individual packing credit cover for each of its individual clients.

2) Whole Turnover Packing Credit Insurance Policy

This policy provides protection against the losses that may be incurred in extending packing credit advances. A bank or a financial institution is eligible to obtain this whole turnover cover for all its accounts.

3) Branch Wise Packing Credit Insurance Policy

A branch of a bank or a financial institution authorized to deal in foreign exchange can obtain the Branch-wise Packing Credit Cover in respect of one or more of its exporter clients.

4) Individual Export Credit Insurance for Banks with Exclusion

Any bank or financial institution who is an authorized dealer in foreign exchange can obtain the Individual Post-shipment Export Credit Cover in respect of its exporter client who is holding the appropriate Comprehensive Risks Policy of ECGC but with specific exclusions. All post-shipment advances given through purchase, negotiation or discount of export bills or advances against bills sent on collection are eligible under the policy.

5) Individual Export Credit Insurance for Banks without Exclusion

Any bank or financial institution who is an authorized dealer in foreign exchange can obtain the Individual Post-shipment Export Credit Cover in respect of each of its exporter-clients who is holding the Standard Policy of ECGC without any exclusion.

6) Individual Post Shipment Insurance for Non-Policy Holders

Any bank or financial institution who is an authorized dealer in foreign exchange can obtain the Individual Post-shipment Export Credit Cover in respect of each of its exporter-clients who is not holding the Standard Policy of the company.

7) Individual Post Shipment Insurance against LC

Any bank or financial institution who is an authorized dealer in foreign exchange can obtain the Individual Post-shipment Export Credit Cover in respect of each of its exporter-clients who is holding the appropriate Comprehensive Risks Policy of ECGC excluding cover for shipments made against L/Cs.

8) Whole Turnover Insurance Policy

A bank or a financial institution dealing with foreign exchange is eligible to obtain this Whole-turnover Cover for all its accounts.

9) Export Finance Insurance Policy

Any bank authorized to deal in foreign exchange can obtain the Export Finance Cover in respect of its exporter-client who has been classified as a standard asset and whose Credit Rating is acceptable to export credit guarantee corporation.

10) Individual Packing Credit Policy

Packing credit cover can be obtained by the bank that provides advances/credit facilities to the exporters for the purposes of manufacturing, processing, purchasing and/ or packing of goods granted by banks to exporters who enter into contracts for export of services or undertaking construction works abroad. The cover provides protection to the banks against losses suffered on account of nonpayment of advances/credit facilities due to insolvency and/ or default of the borrower exporter.

11) Individual Post-shipment Credit Insurance Policy

Any bank or financial institution who is an authorized dealer in foreign exchange that provides post-shipment finance to the exporter by way of purchase, negotiation or discount of export bills after the shipment has been affected pertaining to a particular project.

12) Export Performance Credit Insurance Policy

The cover provides protection to the banks against losses that it may suffer due to insolvency and/ or protracted default of the borrower. Covers can be obtained for each Bank Guarantees issued by the Bank at various stages of the contract.

13) Overseas Lending Credit Insurance Policy

If a bank financing an overseas project provides a foreign currency loan to the contractor, it can protect itself from the risk of non-payment by the contractor by obtaining Export Finance (Overseas Lending) Guarantee.

14) Cash Flow Deficit Financing Credit Insurance Policy

The banks or financial institutions lend money to the contractor to overcome cash flow deficits to ensure smooth and timely execution of the project. This policy provides protection to the banks against losses that bank may suffer due to insolvency and default of the borrower.

Export Credit Insurance Special Schemes

Various special insurance schemes provided by the organization are described below:

1. Buyer Credit Cover Policy

Buyer's Credit is a credit extended by a bank in India to an overseas buyer enabling the buyer to pay for machinery and equipment that he may be importing from India for a specific project. A Line of Credit is a credit extended by a bank in India to an overseas bank or institution or government for the purpose of facilitating import. This policy is designed to protect the lending banks from certain risks of non-payment.

2. Lines of Credit Cover

A Line of Credit is a credit extended by a bank in India to an overseas bank, institution or government for the purpose of facilitating import of a variety of listed goods from India into the overseas country. A number of importers in the overseas country may be importing the goods under one Line of Credit and this scheme is meant to protect the lending banks from certain risks of non-payment.

3. Transfer Guarantee Insurance Cover

When a bank in India adds its confirmation to a foreign Letter of Credit, it binds itself to honor the drafts drawn by the beneficiary of the Letter of Credit without any recourse to him provided such drafts are drawn strictly in accordance with the terms of the Letter of Credit. The confirming bank will suffer a loss if the foreign bank fails to reimburse it with the amount paid to the exporter. The Transfer Guarantee seeks to safeguard banks in India against losses arising out of such risks.

4. Overseas Investment Insurance

This policy is meant to provide protection to the Indian investments abroad. The investment may be either in cash or in the form of export of Indian capital goods and services. The cover would be available for the original investment together with annual dividends or interest receivable. The risks of war, expropriation and restriction on remittances are covered under the scheme.

5. Customer Specific Insurance Cover Policy

In order to cater to the specific need for export credit insurance cover, of reputed large value exporters which otherwise could not be fully addressed under any one of standard products, the customer specific policies have been introduced and are issued to large exporters on a selective basis on the merits respective requests for such cover.

Various Guarantees Offered by ECGC

1. Packing Credit Guarantee

It helps the exporter to obtain better and adequate facilities from their bankers. The Guarantees assure the banks that, in the event of an exporter failing to discharge his liabilities to the bank, ECGC would make good a major portion of the bank's loss. bank is required to be co-insurer to the extent of the remaining loss. Any loan given to an exporter for the manufacture, processing, purchasing or packing of goods meant for export against a firm order or Letter of Credit qualifies for Packing Credit Guarantee. Pre-shipment advances given by banks to parties who enter into contracts for export of services or for construction works abroad to meet preliminary expenses in connection with such contracts are also eligible for cover under the Guarantee. The Guarantee, issued for a period of 12 months based on a proposal from the bank, covers all the advances that may be made by the bank during the period to an individual exporter within an approved limit. Whole-turnover Packing Credit Guarantee (WTPCG) can be issued to banks which wish to obtain cover for packing credit advances granted to all its customers on all-India basis. Premiums are lower and higher percentage of cover is offered under this option.

2. Export Production Finance Guarantee

The purpose of this Guarantee is to enable banks to sanction advances at the pre-shipment stage to the full extent of cost of production when it exceeds the f.o.b. value of the contract/order, the differences representing incentive/duty drawback receivable.

3. Post-Shipment Credit Guarantee

Banks extend post-shipment finance to exporters through purchase, negotiation or discount of export bills or advances against such bills. The post shipment credit guarantee provides protection to banks against non-realisation of export proceeds and the resultant failure of the exporter to repay the advances availed. Individual Post-Shipment Credit Guarantee can also be obtained for finance granted against L/C bills, even where an exporter does not hold an ECGC Policy, provided that the exporter makes shipments solely against Letters of Credit. This guarantee can also be issued on whole turnover basis wherein the percentage of cover under shall be 90% for advances granted to exporters holding ECGC policy. Advances to non-policyholders are also covered with the percentage of cover being 65.

4. Export Finance Guarantee

This guarantee covers post-shipment advances granted by banks to exporters against export incentives receivable in the form of cash assistance, duty drawback, etc.

5. Export Performance Guarantee

This is akin to a counter-guarantee to protect a bank against losses that it may suffer on account of guarantees given by it on behalf of exporters. In the case of bid bonds relating to exports on medium/long term credit, overseas projects, and projects in India financed by international financial institutions as well as supplies to such projects, guarantee is granted on payment of 25% of the prescribed premium. The balance of 75% becomes payable by the bankers if the exporter succeeds in the bid and gets the contract. Exporters are sometimes called upon to execute bonds duly guaranteed by an Indian bank at various stages of export business. An exporter who desires to quote for a foreign tender may have to furnish a bank guarantee in the form of a bid bond. If he wins the contract, he may have to furnish bank guarantees to foreign buyers to ensure due performance or against advance payment or in lieu of retention money or to a foreign bank in case he has to raise overseas finance for his contract. Further, for obtaining import licenses for raw materials or capital goods, exporters may have to execute an undertaking to export goods of a specified value within a stipulated time, duly supported by bank guarantees. Bank guarantees are also furnished by exporters to the Customs, Central Excise, or Sales Tax authorities for the purpose of clearing goods without payment of duty or for exemption from tax for goods procured for export. Exporters may also be required to furnish guarantees in support of export obligations to Export Promotion Councils, Commodity Boards, State Trading Corporation of India, etc.

6. Export Finance (Overseas Lending) Guarantee

Its protects the banks providing foreign currency loans to the contractors executing overseas project, against the risk of non-payment by the contractor. This guarantee indemnifies the insured bank for any loss due to the insolvency or default of the foreign bank opening Letter of Credit or due to certain political risks such as war, transfer delays or moratorium, which may delay or prevent the transfer of funds to the bank in India.

7. Transfer Guarantee

This guarantee seeks to safeguard the banks on the confirmation they might add to letters of credit opened by banks abroad in favour of the Indian exporters. The guarantee covers risks of:

1. Insolvency of the opening bank;
2. Failure of the opening bank to pay within four months from the due date of payment;
3. Operation of law which prevents restricts or controls transfer of the amount
4. Occurrence of war between the country of opening bank and India; and
5. Occurrence of war, hostilities, civil war, rebellion, insurrection or other disturbances in the country of the opening bank.

Benefits of ECGC

Benefits to Banks

1. The maturity factoring facility offered by ECGC does not disturb the existing system of banking arrangement.
2. Banks would be able to finance against the factored bills at zero risk, as they would be protected even in case where the non-payment is due to dispute between the exporter and the buyer.
3. As the discounting of the bill under the scheme is to be done by the exporter's bank they would not face any hassle in adjusting advances granted at the packing credit stage.

Benefits to Exporters

1. 100% risk protection in respect of transactions where the buyer accepts the bills/documents without recourse to the exporter.
2. Sharing of loss in case of non-acceptance of goods/documents due to insolvency or financial difficulty.
3. Receivable management and sales ledger maintenance.
4. Enables the exporter to avail bank finance on easier terms.
5. The exporter can avail of the above benefits without disturbing existing system of banking arrangements.

World Trade Organisation (WTO)

Introduction

The World Trade Organisation came into existence with effect from 1st January 1995.The Uruguay round of GATT (1986-93) gave birth to World Trade Organization. The WTO replaced General Agreement on Tariffs and Trade. It is wider in scope. The members of GATT singed on an agreement of Uruguay round in April 1994 in Morocco for establishing a new organization named WTO. It was officially constituted on January 1, 1995 which took the place of GATT as an effective formal, organization. GATT was an informal organization which regulated world trade since 1948. Contrary to the temporary nature of GATT, WTO is a permanent organization which has been established on the basis of an international treaty approved by participating countries. It achieved the international status like IMF and IBRD, but it is not an agency of the United Nations Organization (UNO).

Structure

The WTO has nearly 153 members accounting for over 97% of world trade. Around 30 others are negotiating membership. Decisions are made by the entire membership. This is typically by consensus. A majority vote is also possible but it has never been used in the WTO and was extremely rare under the WTO's predecessor, GATT. The WTO's agreements have been ratified in all members' parliaments.

The WTO's top level decision-making body is the Ministerial Conferences which meets at least once in every two years. Below this is the General Council which meets several times a year in the Geneva headquarters. The General Council also meets as the Trade Policy Review Body and the Disputes Settlement Body.

At the next level, the Goods Council, Services Council and Intellectual Property (TRIPs) Council report to the General Council. Numerous specialized committees, working groups and working parties deal with the individual agreements and other areas such as, the environment, development, membership applications and regional trade agreements.

Secretariat

The WTO secretariat, based in Geneva, has around 600 staff and is headed by a Director-General. Its annual budget is roughly 160 million Swiss Francs. It does not have branch offices outside Geneva. Since decisions are taken by the members themselves, the secretariat does not have the decision making the role that other international bureaucracies are given. The secretariat' s main duties are to supply technical support for the various councils and committees and the ministerial conferences, to provide technical assistance for developing countries, to analyze world trade and to explain WTO affairs to the public and media. The secretariat also provides some forms of legal assistance in the dispute settlement process and advises governments wishing to become members of the WTO.

Objectives

The Important Objectives of WTO are

1. To improve the standard of living of people in the member countries.
2. To ensure full employment and broad increase in effective demand.
3. To enlarge production and trade of goods.
4. To increase the trade of services.
5. To ensure optimum utilization of world resources.
6. To protect the environment.
7. To accept the concept of sustainable development.
8. To implement the new world trade system as visualized in the Agreement;
9. To promote World Trade in a manner that benefits every country;
10. To demolish all hurdles to an open world trading system
11. To enhance competitiveness among all trading partners

Functions

The former GATT was not really an organisation; it was merely a legal arrangement. On the other hand, the WTO is a new international organisation set up as a permanent body. It is designed to play the role of a watchdog in the spheres of trade in goods, trade in services, foreign investment, intellectual property rights, etc. Article III has set out the following functions of WTO;

- To implement rules and provisions related to trade policy review mechanism.
- To provide a platform to member countries to decide future strategies related to trade and tariff.
- To provide facilities for implementation, administration and operation of multilateral and bilateral agreements of the world trade.
- To administer the rules and processes related to dispute settlement.
- To ensure the optimum use of world resources.

- To assist international organizations such as, IMF and IBRD for establishing coherence in Universal Economic Policy determination.

- The WTO shall provide the forum for negotiations among its members concerning their multilateral trade relations

- With a view to achieving greater coherence in global economic policy making, the WTO shall cooperate, as appropriate, with the international Monetary Fund (IMF) and with the International Bank for Reconstruction and Development (IBRD) and its affiliated agencies.

- To improve the level of living for the global population and speed up economic development of the member nations.

Core Principles of WTO

The WTO aims to achieve its objectives by reducing existing barriers to trade and by preventing new ones from developing. It seeks to ensure fair and equal competitive conditions for market access, and predictability of access for all traded goods and services. This approach is based on following fundamental principles:

1. Principle of National-treatment

The principle of national treatment requires, in its simplest terms that the goods and services of other countries be treated in the same way as those of your own country.

2. Most-favoured Nation Principle

The most-favoured nation principle requires that if special treatment is given to the goods and services of one country, they must be given to all WTO member countries. No one country should receive favour that distorts trade.

3. Sustainable Development

Some argue that the concept of sustainable development has now emerged as a principle to guide the interpretation of the WTO Agreements, though not at the level of the core principles of non-discrimination. In the 1998 Appellate Body ruling in the so-called shrimp-turtle case, it was made clear that the interpretation of WTO law should reflect the Uruguay Round's deliberate inclusion of the language and concept of sustainable development. This ruling may have moved the WTO toward requiring the legal provisions of its agreements to be interpreted and applied in light of the principles and legal standards of sustainable development.

4. Non-discrimination

A country should not discriminate between its trading partners and it should not discriminate between its own and foreign products, services or nationals.

5. More Open

Lowering trade barriers is one of the most obvious ways of encouraging trade; these barriers include customs duties (or tariffs) and measure such as import bans or quotas that restrict quantities selectively.

6. Predictable and Transparent

Foreign companies, investors and governments should be confident that trade barriers should not be raised arbitrarily. With stability and predictability, investment is encouraged, jobs are created and consumers can fully enjoy the benefits of competition — choice and lower prices.

7. More Competitive

Discouraging 'unfair' practices, such as export subsidies and dumping products at below cost to gain market share; the issues are complex, and the rules try to establish what is fair or unfair, and how governments can respond, in particular by charging additional import duties calculated to compensate for damage caused by unfair trade.

8. More Beneficial for Less Developed Countries

Giving them more time to adjust, greater flexibility and special privileges; over three-quarters of WTO members are developing countries and countries in transition to market economies. The WTO agreements give them transition periods to adjust to the more unfamiliar and, perhaps, difficult WTO provisions.

9. Protect the Environment

The WTO's agreements permit members to take measures to protect not only the environment but also public health, animal health and plant health. However, these measures must be applied in the same way to both national and foreign businesses. In other words, members must not use environmental protection measures as a means of disguising protectionist policies.

Main Activities of WTO

While the WTO is driven by its member states, it could not function without its Secretariat to coordinate the activities. The Secretariat employs over 600 staff and its experts — lawyers, economists, statisticians and communications experts — assist WTO members on a daily basis to ensure, among other things, that negotiations progress smoothly, and that the rules of international trade are correctly applied and enforced.

1. Trade Negotiations

The WTO agreements cover goods, services and intellectual property. They spell out the principles of liberalization, and the permitted exceptions. They include individual countries' commitments to lower customs tariffs and other trade barriers, and to open and keep open services markets. They set procedures for settling disputes. These agreements are not static; they are renegotiated from time to time and new agreements can be added to the package. Negotiating in the reduction or elimination of obstacles to trade (import tariffs, other barriers to trade) and agreeing on rules governing the conduct of international trade

2. Implementation and Monitoring

WTO agreements require governments to make their trade policies transparent by notifying the WTO about laws in force and measures adopted. Various WTO councils and committees seek to ensure that these requirements are being followed and that WTO agreements are being properly implemented. All WTO members must undergo periodic scrutiny of their trade policies and practices, each review containing reports by the country concerned and the WTO Secretariat. It also administers and monitor the application of the WTO's agreed rules for trade in goods, trade in services and trade-related intellectual property rights. WTO reviews the trade policies of members and ensures transparency of regional and bilateral trade agreements.

3. Dispute Settlement

The WTO's procedure for resolving trade quarrels under the Dispute Settlement Understanding is vital for enforcing the rules and therefore for ensuring that trade flows smoothly. Countries bring disputes to the WTO if they think their rights under the agreements are being infringed. Judgments by specially appointed independent experts are based on interpretations of the agreements and individual countries' commitments.

4. Building Trade Capacity

WTO agreements contain special provision for developing countries, including longer time periods to implement agreements and commitments, measures to increase their trading opportunities, and support to help them build their trade capacity, to handle disputes and to implement technical standards. The WTO organizes hundreds of technical cooperation missions to developing countries annually. It also holds numerous courses each year in Geneva for government officials. Aid for Trade aims to help developing countries develop the skills and infrastructure needed to expand their trade.

5. Outreach

The WTO maintains regular dialogue with non-governmental organizations, parliamentarians, other international organizations, the media and the general public on various aspects of the WTO and the ongoing Doha negotiations, with the aim of enhancing cooperation and increasing awareness of WTO activities.

6. Conducting Research

The WTO is assisting the process of accession of some 30 countries who are not yet members of the organization. It conducts economic research and collecting and disseminating trade data in support. It educates the public about the WTO, its mission and its activities.

The Benefits of WTO

1. The System Helps Promote Peace

This sounds like an exaggerated claim, and it would be wrong to make too much of it. Nevertheless, the system does contribute to international peace, and if we understand why, we have a clearer picture of what the system actually does.

2. Disputes are Handled Constructively

As trade expands in volume, in the number of products traded, and in the numbers of countries and companies trading, there is a greater chance that disputes will arise. The WTO system helps resolve these disputes peacefully and constructively.

3. Rules make Life Easier for All

The WTO cannot claim to make all countries equal. But it does reduce some inequalities, giving smaller countries more voice, and at the same time freeing the major powers from the complexity of having to negotiate trade agreements with each of their numerous trading partners.

4. Free Trade Cuts the Costs of Living

The WTO's global system lowers trade barriers through negotiation and applies the principle of non- discrimination. The result is reduced costs of production (because imports used in production are cheaper) and reduced prices of finished goods and services, and ultimately a lower cost of living.

5. It Provides More Choice of Products and Qualities

The wider choice isn't simply a question of consumers buying foreign finished products. Imports are used as materials, components and equipment for local production. This expands the range of final products and services that are made by domestic producers, and it increases the range of technologies they can use. When mobile telephone equipment became available, services sprang up even in the countries that did not make the equipment.

6. Trade Raises Incomes

Lowering trade barriers allows trade to increase, which adds to incomes — national incomes and personal incomes. Trade also poses challenges as domestic producers face competition from imports. But the fact that there is additional income means that resources are available for governments to redistribute the benefits from those who gain the most.

7. Trade Stimulates Economic Growth

Trade clearly has the potential to create jobs. In practice there is often factual evidence that lower trade barriers have been good for employment. Careful policy-making harnesses the job-creation powers of freer trade

8. The Basic Principles make Life More Efficient

Many of the benefits of the trading system are more difficult to summarize in numbers, but they are still important. They are the result of essential principles at the heart of the system, and they make life simpler for the enterprises directly involved in trade and for the producers of goods and services. Trade allows a division of labour between countries. It allows resources to be used more appropriately and effectively for production. But the WTO's trading system offers more than that. It helps to increase efficiency and to cut costs even more because of important principles enshrined in the system.

9. Governments are Shielded from Lobbying

The GATT-WTO system which evolved in the second half of the 20th Century helps governments take a more balanced view of trade policy. Governments are better-placed to defend themselves against lobbying from narrow interest groups by focusing on trade-offs that are made in the interests of everyone in the economy. One of the lessons of the protectionism that dominated the early decades of the 20th Century was the damage that can be caused if narrow Sectoral interests gain an unbalanced share of political influence. The result was increasingly restrictive policy which turned into a trade war that no one won and everyone lost.

10. The System Encourages Good Government

Under WTO rules, once a commitment has been made to liberalize a sector of trade, it is difficult to reverse. The rules also discourage a range of unwise policies. For businesses, that means greater certainty and clarity about trading conditions. For governments it can often mean good discipline. The rules include commitments not to backslide into unwise policies. Protectionism in general is unwise because of the damage it causes domestically and internationally, as we have already seen. Particular types of trade barriers cause additional damage because they provide opportunities for corruption and other forms of bad government.

INTERNATIONAL MONETARY FUND (IMF)

Introduction

During the Bretton Woods Conference, a lot of agreements were signed to legally establish the General Agreement on Tariffs & Trade (GATT), the International Bank for Reconstruction & Development (World Bank or IBRD) and the International Monetary Fund (IMF). The International Monetary Fund was founded on 27th December, 1945. The financial operations of the IMF started on 1st March, 1947. The primary purpose of the International Monetary Fund is to give technical and financial assistance, oversee exchange rates, and address global financial problems. Currently, the International Monetary Fund has 182 member countries. In order to be a member of the IMF, countries need to deposit a specific amount of money as subscription fee. The countries also need to comply with the terms and conditions of the organization. The IMF was founded more than 60 years ago and the founders aimed to build a framework for economic cooperation that would avoid a repetition of the disastrous economic policies that had contributed to the Great Depression of the 1930s and the global conflict that followed. Since then the world has changed dramatically, bringing extensive prosperity and lifting millions out of poverty, especially in Asia.

The IMF has gone through two distinct phases in its 50-year history. During the first phase, ending in 1973, the IMF oversaw the adoption of general convertibility among the major currencies, supervised a system of fixed exchange rates tied to the value of gold, and provided short-term financing to countries in need of a quick infusion of foreign exchange to keep their currencies at par value or to adjust to changing economic circumstances. Difficulties encountered in maintaining a system of fixed exchange rates gave rise to unstable monetary and financial conditions throughout the world and led the international community to reconsider how the IMF could most effectively function in a regime of flexible exchange rates. After five years of analysis and negotiation (1973-78), the IMF's second phase began with the amendment of its constitution in 1978, broadening its functions to enable it to grapple with the challenges that have arisen since the collapse of the par value system.

Aims of IMF

The Important Aims of IMF are as under

- Main aim is to provide the global public good of financial stability.
- Provide a forum for cooperation on international monetary problems
- Facilitate the growth of international trade, thus promoting job creation, economic

* growth, and poverty reduction;
* Promote exchange rate stability and an open system of international payments; and
* Lend countries foreign exchange when needed, on a temporary basis and under
* adequate safeguards, to help them address balance of payments problems.

Key Activities of IMF

The IMF supports its membership by providing the followings.

* Policy advice to governments and central banks based on analysis of economic trends and cross-country experiences;
* Research, statistics, forecasts, and analysis based on tracking of global, regional, and individual economies and markets;
* Loans to help countries overcome economic difficulties;
* Concessional loans to help fight poverty in developing countries; and
* Technical assistance and training to help countries improve the management of their economies.

Functions of IMF

IMF Performs the following Functions

1. Responding to the Global Economic Crisis

The IMF responded quickly to the global economic crisis, with lending commitments reaching a record level of more than US$250 billion in 2010. This figure includes a sharp increase in concessional lending (that's to say, subsidized lending at rates below those being charged by the market) to the world's poorest nations.

2. Broader Financial Safety

The IMF has overhauled its lending framework to make it better suited to countries' individual needs. It is also working with other regional institutions to create a broader financial safety net, which could help prevent new crises.

3. Policy Advice

The IMF's monitoring, forecasts, and policy advice, informed by a global perspective and by experience from previous crises, have been in high demand and have been used by the G-20.

4. Lessons from the Crisis

The IMF is contributing to the ongoing effort to draw lessons from the crisis for policy, regulation, and reform of the global financial architecture.

5. Preserving the Voice of the Low-income Members

The IMF's member countries also agreed to a significant increase in the voice of dynamic emerging and developing economies in the decision making of the institution, while preserving the voice of the low-income members.

6. Free Exchange

IMF continues to urge its members to allow their national currencies to be exchanged without restriction for the currencies of other member countries.

7. Supervision

IMF supervises economic policies that influence their balance of payments in the presently legalized flexible exchange rate environment. This supervision provides opportunities for an early warning of any exchange rate or balance of payments problem.

8. Apprising Potential Problems

It confers at regular intervals (usually once a year) with its members, analyzing their economic positions and apprising them of actual or potential problems arising from their policies, and keeps the entire membership informed of these developments.

9. Financial Assistance

The IMF continues to provide short- and medium-term financial assistance to member nations that run into temporary balance of payments difficulties. The financial assistance usually involves the provision by the IMF of convertible currencies to augment the afflicted member's dwindling foreign exchange reserves.

10. Raising the Competitiveness of Exports

In a collaborative effort, the country and the IMF can attempt to root out the causes of the payments imbalance by working out a comprehensive program that, depending on the particulars of the case, might include raising producer prices paid to farmers so as to encourage agricultural production and reverse migration to the cities, lowering interest rates to expand the supply of credit, and adjusting the currency to reflect the level of world prices, thereby discouraging imports and raising the competitiveness of exports.

11. Technical Assistance

The IMF also helps by providing technical assistance in organizing central banks, establishing and reforming tax systems, and setting up agencies to gather and publish economic statistics.

12. Special Drawing Rights

The IMF is also authorized to issue a special type of money, called the SDR, to provide its members with additional liquidity. Known technically as a fiduciary asset, the SDR can be retained by members as part of their monetary reserves or be used in place of national currencies in transactions with other members.

13. Supervision of Members' Economic Policies

In response to an emerging interest by the world community to return to a more stable system of exchange rates that would reduce the present fluctuations in the values of currencies, the IMF has been strengthening its supervision of members' economic policies.

Special Drawing Rights (SDRs)

The SDR was created as a result of the First Amendment of the Articles of Agreement, which became effective in 1969. It was created as a supplement to existing reserve assets as the demand for reserves was expected to grow substantially over time in line with growing world trade. 80 Specifically, there were concerns that the growth in the supply of reserves (which comprised mainly gold and the U.S. dollar) would be insufficient since it depended on a diminishing supply of newly-mined gold entering into official reserves and on continued and unsustainable deficits in the balance of payments of the United States. It was also thought that U.S. gold stocks would decline relative to U.S. dollar liabilities, which would eventually make the par value of the U.S. dollar relative to gold unsustainable and precipitate an international monetary crisis. The intention was therefore to establish the SDR system to expand world reserves independently of the growth of official holdings of gold and foreign exchange. Further changes to the SDR system came about as a result of the Second Amendment of the Articles of Agreement, which had as an objective to make the SDR the principal reserve asset in the international monetary system. The SDR is also the unit of account that is used by the IMF. However, the role of the SDR as a reserve asset has been very limited and SDRs currently comprise only a small fraction of members' international reserves. To date, only two series of SDR allocations have been made, totaling SDR 21.4 billion. International monetary conditions did not evolve as envisaged at the time of creation of the SDR. The Bretton Woods par value system broke down in the early 1970s and was replaced by a system of managed floating exchange rates. Furthermore, the growth of international capital markets meant that many countries could augment their international reserves through borrowing. Consequently, a shortage of international reserves did not materialize as expected. In addition, the SDR can only be held by official entities or approved official holders, and used in official transactions and operations. While these factors limited the role of the SDR as a reserve asset, the SDR helps lower the cost of holding reserves by reducing the need for borrowed reserves.

Main Characteristics of the SDR System

1. Separation of SDR and GRA Accounts

All operations and transactions involving Special Drawing Rights are conducted through a Special Drawing Rights Department. All other operations and transactions on account of the IMF, including those involving the use of IMF resources, are conducted through the General Department. Assets held in the SDR Department are not available to finance the operations of the General Department, and vice-versa, except that the General Department pays the expenses of conducting the business of the SDR Department and is reimbursed in Special Drawing Rights by the SDR Department. Separate financial statements are produced for the two departments. Holders of Special Drawing Rights.

All IMF members have chosen to participate in the SDR Department. Participants receive allocations of Special Drawing Rights, may hold or use Special Drawing Rights. The IMF and prescribed holders acquire and use Special Drawing Rights through transactions with participants and with each other. The IMF receives and disburses Special Drawing Rights in transactions conducted through the General Resources Account (GRA), and holds Special Drawing Rights in the GRA. Sources of IMF holdings include quota subscriptions, repurchases, interest on loans to members and on GRA holdings, and re-imbursements for the cost of conducting the business of the SDR Department. Uses of Special Drawing Rights by the IMF include purchases, remuneration on members' creditor positions, repayments of and interest on IMF borrowing, and acquisition by members to pay charges and assessments.

2. Allocation and Cancellation of Special Drawing Rights

Decisions on the allocation and cancellation of Special Drawing Rights are usually made for successive basic periods of five years each. To date there has not been any cancellation. Decisions to allocate Special Drawing Rights are based on a judgment that a long-term global need to augment international liquidity exists, and require approval by an 85 percent majority of the total voting power of the SDR Department. A participant that votes against the allocation or notifies the IMF that it does not wish to receive any allocation will not participate in the allocation. The IMF cannot allocate Special Drawing Rights to itself or to other prescribed official holders. Allocations or cancellations within a basic period take place at yearly intervals, although the IMF can decide to put in place other intervals. Members who become participants after a basic period starts receive allocations beginning with the next basic period in which allocations are made, unless the IMF decides that the new participant shall start to receive allocations beginning with the next allocation within the current basic period. A proposal for a special one-time allocation of Special Drawing Rights was approved by the IMF's Board of Governors in September 1997 through the proposed Fourth Amendment of the Articles of Agreement. 82 This amendment has not yet entered into effect. The allocation would double cumulative SDR allocations to SDR 42.8 billion. Its intent is to enable all members of the IMF to participate in the SDR system on an equitable basis and correct for the fact that countries that joined the IMF subsequent to 1981— more than one fifth of the current IMF membership— have never received an SDR allocation. The Fourth Amendment will become effective when three fifths of the IMF membership (111 members) with 85 percent of the total voting power accept it. As of end October, 2006, 131 members with 77.3 percent of total voting power had accepted the proposed amendment. Approval by the United States is necessary to put the amendment into effect.

Use of Special Drawing Rights

1. The SDR serves as the unit of account of the IMF and a number of other international organizations.
2. In addition to financial assistance, the IMF also provides member countries with technical assistance to create and implement effective policies, particularly economic, monetary, and banking policy and regulations.
3. A Special Drawing Right is basically an international monetary reserve asset. Special Drawing Rights were created in 1969 by the IMF in response to the Triffin Paradox. The Triffin Paradox stated that the more US dollars were used as a base reserve currency, the less faith that countries had in the ability of the US government to convert those dollars to gold.
4. Special Drawing Right would replace the US dollar as the global monetary reserve currency, thus solving the Triffin Paradox. Bretton Woods collapsed a few years later, but the concept of an SDR solidified.
5. The SDR is not a currency, but some refer to it as a form of IMF currency, which provide a mechanism for buying, selling, and exchanging Special Drawing Rights.
6. Special Drawing Rights can be exchanged between countries along with currencies.

Opportunities and Future Outlook for the IMF

The 2008 global economic crisis is one of the toughest situations that the IMF has had to contend with since the Great Depression. For most of the first decade of the twenty-first century, global trade and finance fueled a global expansion that enabled many countries to repay any money they had borrowed from the IMF and other official creditors. These countries also used surpluses in trade to accumulate foreign exchange reserves. The global economic crisis that began with the 2007 collapse of mortgage lending in the United States and spread around the world in 2008 was preceded by large imbalances in global capital flows. Global capital flows fluctuated between 2 and 6 percent of world GDP between 1980 and 1995, but since then they have risen to 15 percent of GDP. The most rapid increase has been experienced by advanced economies, but emerging markets and developing countries have also become more financially integrated. The founders of the Bretton Woods system had taken for granted that private capital flows would never again resume the prominent role they had in the nineteenth and early twentieth centuries, and the IMF had traditionally lent to members facing current account difficulties. The 2008 global crisis uncovered fragility in the advanced financial markets that soon led to the worst global downturn since the Great Depression.

Suddenly, the IMF was inundated with requests for standby arrangements and other forms of financial and policy support.

The international community recognized that the IMF's financial resources were as important as ever and were likely to be stretched thin before the crisis was over. With broad support from creditor countries, the IMF's lending capacity tripled to around $750 billion. To use those funds effectively, the IMF overhauled its lending policies. It created a flexible credit line for countries with strong economic fundamentals and a track record of successful policy implementation. Other reforms targeted low-income countries. These factors enabled the IMF to disburse very large sums quickly; the disbursements were based on the needs of borrowing countries and were not as tightly constrained by quotas as in the past.

Strengths and Opportunities of IMF

The IMF's requirements are not always popular but are usually effective, which has led to its expanding influence. The IMF has sought to correct some of the criticisms; according to a Foreign Policy in Focus essay designed to stimulate dialogue on the IMF, the fund's strengths and opportunities include the following:

1. Flexibility and Speed

In March 2009, the IMF created the Flexible Credit Line, which is a fast-disbursing loan facility with low conditionality aimed at reassuring investors by injecting liquidity. Traditionally, IMF loan programs require the imposition of austerity measures such as raising interest rates that can reduce foreign investment...In the case of the FCL, countries qualify for it not on the basis of their promises, but on the basis of their history. Just as individual borrowers with good credit histories are eligible for loans at lower interest rates than their risky counterparts, similarly, countries with sound macroeconomic fundamentals are eligible for drawings under the FCL. A similar program has been proposed for low-income countries. Known as the Rapid Credit Facility, it is front-loaded (allowing for a single, up-front payout as with the FCL) and is also intended to have low conditionality.

2. Cheerleading

The Fund is positioning itself to be less of an adversary and more of a cheerleader to member countries. For some countries that need loans more for reassurance than reform, these changes to the Fund toolkit are welcome. This enables more domestic political and economic stability.

3.Adaptability

Instead of providing the same medicine to all countries regardless of their particular problems, the new loan facilities are intended to aid reform-minded governments by providing short-term resources to reassure investors. In this manner, they help politicians in developing countries manage the downside costs of integration.

4. Transparency

The IMF has made efforts to improve its own transparency and continues to encourage its member countries to do so. Supporters note that this creates a barrier to any one or more countries that have more geopolitical influence in the organization. In reality, the major economies continue to exert influence on policy and implementation.

Criticism for the IMF

The IMF supports many developing nations by helping them overcome monetary challenges and to maintain a stable international financial system. Despite this clearly defined purpose, the execution of its work can be very complicated and can have wide repercussions for the recipient nations. As a result, the IMF has both its critics and its supporters. The IMF has been subject to a range of criticisms that are generally focused on the conditions of its loans, its lack of accountability, and its willingness to lend to countries with bad human rights records.

These Criticisms Include the Following

1. Conditions for Loans

The IMF makes the loan given to countries conditional on the implementation of certain economic policies, which typically include the following:

Reducing government borrowing (higher taxes and lower spending), higher interest rates to stabilize the currency, Allowing failing firms to go bankrupt and Structural adjustment (privatization, deregulation, reducing corruption and bureaucracy.

2. Exchange Rate Reforms

The IMF failed to understand the dynamics of the country that they were dealing with. When the IMF intervened in Kenya in the 1990s, they made the Central bank remove controls over flows of capital. The consensus was that this decision made it easier for corrupt politicians to transfer money out of the economy.

3. Devaluations

In the initial stages, the IMF has been criticized for allowing inflationary devaluations

4. Free-market Criticisms of the IMF

Believers in free markets argue that it is better to let capital markets operate without attempts at intervention. They argue attempts to influence exchange rates only make things worse—it is better to allow currencies to reach their market level. They also assert that bailing out countries with large debts is morally hazardous; countries that know that there is always a bailout provision will borrow and spend more recklessly.

5. Lack of Transparency and Involvement

The IMF has been criticized for imposing policy with little or no consultation with affected countries.

6. Supporting Military Dictatorships

The IMF has been criticized over the decades for supporting military dictatorships.

EXCHANGE RATE

A mechanism by which the currency of one country gets converted in to the currency of another country is known as exchange rate. The exchange rate is the price of the currency of a country in terms of another currency. An exchange rate thus has two components, the domestic currency and a foreign currency, and can be quoted either directly or indirectly. In a direct quotation, the price of a unit of foreign currency is expressed in terms of the domestic currency. In an indirect quotation, the price of a unit of domestic currency is expressed in terms of the foreign currency. It is the rate at which one currency may be converted into another. The exchange rate is used when simply converting one currency to another (such as for the purposes of travel to another country), or for engaging in speculation or trading in the foreign exchange market.

Types of Exchange Rates

In the foreign exchange market, at a particular time, there exists, not one unique exchange rate, but a variety of rates, depending upon the credit instruments used in the transfer function. Major types of exchange rates are as follows:

Spot Rate

Spot rate of exchange is the rate at which foreign exchange is made available on the spot. The spot exchange rate refers to the current exchange rate. The exchange rate at which two parties agrees to trade two currencies at the present moment. The spot exchange rate is usually at or close to the current market rate because the transaction occurs in real time and not at some point in the future. Some analysts believe that forward rates are an accurate predictor of future spot rates, though many others dispute this. It is also known as cable rate or telegraphic transfer rate because at this rate cable or telegraphic sale and purchase of foreign exchange can be arranged immediately. Spot rate is the day-to-day rate of exchange. A spot contract is a contract that involves the purchase or sale of a commodity, security or currency for immediate delivery and payment on the spot date, which is normally two business days after the trade date. The spot rate, or spot price, is the price quoted for the immediate settlement of the spot contract. For example, say an investor believes orange juice is more expensive in the winter due to supply and demand. However, the investor cannot buy a spot contract for delivery in December because the commodity will spoil. A forward contract is a better fit for the investment.

Forward Rate

Forward rate of exchange is the rate at which the future contract for foreign currency is made. The forward exchange rate is settled now but the actual sale and purchase of foreign exchange occurs in future. The forward rate is quoted at a premium or discount over the spot rate. It refers to an exchange rate that is quoted and traded today but for delivery and payment on a specific future date. A transaction in which two parties agree to trade two currencies at a given exchange rate at some, stated point in the future. That is, the actual trade occurs at the agreed-upon exchange rate, regardless of what the spot rate is when the transaction takes place. It is a type of forward contract and is used to hedge against foreign exchange risk. A forward contract is a contract that involves an agreement of contract terms on the current date with the delivery and payment at a specified future date. Contrary to a spot rate, a forward rate is used to quote a financial transaction that takes place on a future date and is the settlement price of a forward contract. However, depending on the security being traded, the forward rate can be calculated using the spot rate.

Fixed Exchange Rate

Fixed or pegged exchange rate refers to the system in which the rate of exchange of a currency is fixed or pegged in terms of gold or another currency. It is otherwise known as Pegged Rate. This occurs when the government seeks to keep the value of a currency fixed against another currency. In a fixed exchange rate system, the government intervenes in the currency market in order to keep the exchange rate close to a fixed target. It is committed to a single fixed exchange rate and does not allow major fluctuations from this central rate.

Advantages of Fixed Exchange Rates

The main arguments advanced in favor of the system of fixed or stable exchange rates are as follows:

1. Promotes International Trade

Fixed or stable exchange rates ensure certainty about the foreign payments and inspire confidence among the importers and exporters. This helps to promote international trade.

2. Necessary for Small Nations

Fixed exchange rates are even more essential for the smaller nations in whose economies foreign trade plays a dominant role. Fluctuating exchange rates will seriously affect the process of economic growth in these economies.

3. Promotes International Investment

Fixed exchange rates promote international investments. If the exchange rates are fluctuating, the lenders and investors will not be prepared to lend for long-term investments.

4. Removes Speculation

Fixed exchange rates eliminate the speculative activities in the international transactions. There is no possibility of panic flight of capital from one country to another in the system of fixed exchange rates.

5. Necessary for Small Nations

Fixed exchange rates arc even more essential for the smaller nations in whose economies foreign trade plays a dominant role. Fluctuating exchange rates will seriously disturb the process of economic growth of these economies.

6. Necessary for Developing Countries

Fixed exchanges rates are necessary and desirable for the developing countries for carrying out planned development efforts. Fluctuating rates disturb the smooth process of economic development and restrict the inflow of foreign capital.

7. Suitable for Currency Area

A fixed or stable exchange rate system is most suitable to a world of currency areas, such as the sterling area. If the exchange rates of the countries in the common currency area are flexible, the fluctuations in the leading country, like England (whose currency dominates), will also disturb the exchange rates of the whole area.

8. Economic Stabilization

Fixed foreign exchange rate ensures internal economic stabilization and checks unwarranted changes in the prices within the economy. In a system of flexible exchange rates, the liquidity preference is high because the businessmen will like to enjoy wind fall gains from the fluctuating exchange rates. This tends to Increase price and hoarding activities in country.

9. Not Permanently Fixed

Under the fixed exchange rate system, the exchange rate does not remain fixed or is permanently frozen.

Rather the rate is changed at the appropriate time to correct the fundamental disequilibrium in the balance of payments.

Disadvantages of Fixed Exchange Rates

The system of fixed exchange rates has been criticized on the following grounds:

1. Outmoded System

Fixed exchange rate system worked successfully under the favorable conditions of gold standard during 19th century.

2. Discourage Foreign Investment

Fixed exchange rates are not permanently fixed or rigid. Therefore, such a system discourages long- term foreign investment which is considered available under the really fixed exchange rate system.

3. Monetary Dependence

Under the fixed exchange rate system, a country is deprived of its monetary independence. It requires a country to pursue a policy of monetary expansion or contraction in order to maintain stability in its rate of exchange.

4. Cost-Price Relationship not reflected

The fixed exchange rate system does not reflect the true cost-price relationship between the currencies of the countries. No two countries follow the same economic policies. Therefore the cost-price relationship between them goes on changing. If the exchange rate is to reflect the changing cost-price relationship between the countries, it must be flexible.

5. Not a Genuinely Fixed System

The system of fixed exchange rates provides neither the expectation of permanently stable rates as found in the gold standard system, nor the continuous and sensitive adjustment of a freely fluctuating exchange rate.

6. Difficulties of IMF System

The system of fixed or pegged exchange rates, as followed by the International Monetary Fund (IMF), is in reality a system of managed flexibility which involves certain difficulties.

Floating Exchange Rate

Floating rate is otherwise known as flexible exchange rate. Floating exchange rate refers to the system in which the rate of exchange is determined by the forces of demand and supply in the foreign exchange market. It is free to fluctuate according to the changes in the demand and supply of foreign currency. Floating Exchange Rate occurs when the government does not intervene in the foreign exchange market but allows market forces to determine the level of a currency. Unlike the fixed rate, a floating exchange rate is determined by the private market through supply and demand. A floating exchange rate is constantly changing. In reality, no currency is wholly fixed or flexible. The floating rate may be of two namely free floating and managed floating.

a. Free Floating Exchange Rate

The value of the currency is determined solely by supply and demand in the foreign exchange market. Consequently, trade flows and capital flows are the main factors affecting the exchange rate. The definition of a floating exchange rate system is a monetary system in which exchange rates are allowed to move due to market forces without intervention by national governments. The Bank of England, for example, does not actively intervene in the currency markets to achieve a desired exchange rate level. With floating exchange rates, changes in market supply and demand cause a currency to change in value. Pure free floating exchange rates are rare - most governments at one time or another seek to manage the value of their currency through changes in interest rates and other means of controls.

b. Managed Floating Exchange Rates

Most governments engage in managed floating systems, if not part of a fixed exchange rate system. Fluctuations in the exchange rate can provide an automatic adjustment for countries with a large balance of payments deficit. A second key advantage of floating exchange rates is that it allows the government/ monetary authority flexibility in determining interest rates as they do not need to be used to influence the Import Procedures exchange rate.

Advantages of Floating Exchange Rates

1. No Need for International Management of Exchange Rates

Unlike fixed exchange rates based on a metallic standard, floating exchange rates don't require an international manager such as the International Monetary Fund to look over current account imbalances. Under the floating system, if a country has large current account deficits, its currency depreciates.

2. No Need for Frequent Central Bank Intervention

Central banks frequently must intervene in foreign exchange markets under the fixed exchange rate regime to protect the gold parity, but such is not the case under the floating regime. Here there's no parity to uphold.

3. No Need for Elaborate Capital Flow Restrictions

It is difficult to keep the parity intact in a fixed exchange rate regime while portfolio flows are moving in and out of the country. In a floating exchange rate regime, the macroeconomic fundamentals of countries affect the exchange rate in international markets, which, in turn, affect portfolio flows between countries. Therefore, floating exchange rate regimes enhance market efficiency.

4. Greater Insulation from Other Countries' Economic Problems

Under a fixed exchange rate regime, countries export their macroeconomic problems to other countries. Suppose that the inflation rate in the U.S. is rising relative to that of the Euro-zone.

Disadvantages of Floating Exchange Rates

1. Higher Volatility

Floating exchange rates are highly volatile. Additionally, macroeconomic fundamentals can't explain especially short-run volatility in floating exchange rates.

2. Use of Scarce Resources to Predict Exchange Rates

Higher volatility in exchange rates increases the exchange rate risk that financial market participants face. Therefore, they allocate substantial resources to predict the changes in the exchange rate, in an effort to manage their exposure to exchange rate risk.

3. Tendency to Worsen Existing Problems

Floating exchange rates may aggravate existing problems in the economy. If the country is already experiencing economic problems such as higher inflation or unemployment, floating exchange rates may make the situation worse.

4. Multiple Exchange Rates

Multiple rates refer to a system in which a country adopts more than one rate of exchange for its currency. Different exchange rates are fixed for importers, exporters, and for different countries. A system where a country will have both fixed and floating foreign exchange rates at the same time, and both can be used when exchanging currencies in that country. In this situation, the market is divided into any number of segments, each with its own exchange rate. This is frequently used to give preferential treatment to people dealing with goods and products that are the most important to the country; people importing these goods can be given a better exchange rate than people who are importing goods that are not as necessary for the country. If a country only imposes two different exchange rates at the same time, it is referred to as a dual exchange rate system. Two-tier exchange rate system is a form of multiple exchange rate system in which a country maintains two rates, a higher rate for commercial transactions and a lower rate for capital transactions.

Advantages

The main advantages of multiple exchange rates system are as follows;

1. Promotion of Exports
2. Imports become profitable
3. Correcting Balance of Payments deficit
4. Capital formation
5. Capital flows
6. Helpful for weak industries
7. Diversifying the economy
8. Maximizing revenues
9. Favourable terms of trade

Disadvantages

1. Administrative difficulties
2. Discriminatory
3. Harmful for domestic industries
4. Black marketing
5. Less effective in BOP
6. Accumulation of inventories
7. Insufficient system

5. Cross Exchange Rate

The exchange rate between two currencies that are not the official currencies of the country that the exchange was quoted in. Cross rates usually do not involve the U.S. dollar. Cross rate and pip - are two of the main terms in Forex market. Cross-rate is when two currencies are equal which follows from their Forex currency exchange rate according to a Forex rate of the third currency. Pairs of non-US dollar currencies are called "crosses." Cross rates are the current exchange rates between two currencies. The cross rate differs from a currency pair in that a true cross rate must involve two currencies that are not the standard for the country where the evaluation of the exchange rate takes place. By contrast, a currency pair would involve the comparison of the current rate of exchange between the home currency and that of another nation.

Factors which Determine the Exchange Rates

An exchange rate is determined by supply and demand factors. These are the various factors which determine the demand and supply of a currency. Exchange rates play a vital role in a country's level of trade, which is critical to most every free market economy in the world. The following are some of the principal determinants of the exchange rate between two countries.

1. International Trade

Foreign exchange is required primarily for settlement of import and export transactions. In addition to this trade in goods, many invisible items also entail movement of foreign exchange, like rendering of services by residents of one country to that of another, in the form of transport, banking, technical services, etc. When the export of goods and services are increasing, it would mean the demand for the country's currency would increase in the foreign exchange market because importers have to pay in that currency. The increase in demand would make the external value of the currency to rise. Similarly, when imports increase the supply of the country's currency in the foreign exchange market would increase. This will have the effect of fall in the external value of the currency.

2. Differentials in Inflation

As a rule of thumb, a country with a consistently lower inflation rate exhibits a rising currency value, as its purchasing power increases relative to other currencies. During the last half of the twentieth century, the countries with low inflation included Japan, Germany and Switzerland, while the U.S. and Canada achieved low inflation only later. Those countries with higher inflation typically see depreciation in their currency in relation to the currencies of their trading partners. This is also usually accompanied by higher interest rates.

3. Differentials in Interest Rates

Interest rates, inflation and exchange rates are all highly correlated. By manipulating interest rates, central banks exert influence over both inflation and exchange rates, and changing interest rates impact inflation and currency values. Higher interest rates offer lenders in an economy a higher return relative to other countries. Therefore, higher interest rates attract foreign capital and cause the exchange rate to rise. The impact of higher interest rates is mitigated, however, if inflation in the country is much higher than in others, or if additional factors serve to drive the currency down. The opposite relationship exists for decreasing interest rates - that is, lower interest rates tend to decrease exchange rates.

4. Current-account Deficits

The current account is the balance of trade between a country and its trading partners , reflecting all payments between countries for goods, services, interest and dividends. A deficit in the current account shows the country is spending more on foreign trade than it is earning, and that it is borrowing capital from foreign sources to make up the deficit. In other words, the country requires more foreign currency than it receives through sales of exports, and it supplies more of its own currency than foreigners demand for its products. The excess demand for foreign currency lowers the country's exchange rate until domestic goods and services are cheap enough for foreigners, and foreign assets are too expensive to generate sales for domestic interests.

5. Public Debt

Countries will engage in large-scale deficit financing to pay for public sector projects and governmental funding. While such activity stimulates the domestic economy, nations with large public deficits and debts are less attractive to foreign investors. A large debt encourages inflation, and if inflation is high, the debt will be serviced and ultimately paid off with cheaper real dollars in the future. In the worst case scenario, a government may print money to pay part of a large debt, but increasing the money supply inevitably causes inflation. Moreover, if a government is not able to service its deficit through selling domestic bonds, increasing the money supply, then it must increase the supply of securities for sale to foreigners, thereby lowering their prices. Moreover, a large debt may prove worrisome to foreigners if they believe the country risks defaulting on its obligations. Foreigners will be less willing to own securities denominated in that currency if the risk of default is great.

6. Terms of Trade

A ratio comparing export prices to import prices, the terms of trade is related to current accounts and the balance of payments. If the price of a country's exports rises by a greater rate than that of its imports, its terms of trade have favorably improved. This, in turn results in rising revenues from exports which provides increased demand for the currency a country and increase value of the currency. If the price of exports rises by a smaller rate than that of its imports, the currency's value will decrease in relation to its trading partners.

7. Political Stability and Economic Performance

Foreign investors inevitably seek out stable countries with strong economic performance in which to invest their capital. A country with such positive attributes will draw investment funds away from other countries perceived to have more political and economic risk. Political turmoil, for example, can cause a loss of confidence in a currency and a movement of capital to the currencies of more stable countries.

8. Capital Investments

The granting of foreign loan and international dealings in stock exchange would also influence the demand and supply in foreign exchange markets. The industrial climate in the country may be conducive for investors in other countries and induce them to invest in securities of the country. Or, stock exchange transactions may be done for speculation. With good industrial climate and demand for securities the demand for the currency and its value would rise.

9. Interest Rates

The interest rate has a great influence on short-term movement of capital. When the interest rate in a financial centre is higher than the rate prevailing in other centres, it attracts short-term funds from other centres. This would increase the demand for the currency of the centre and hence its value. The movement of huge surplus of OPEC countries from one centre to another to take advantage of interest differential is a good example.

10. Speculation

If speculators believe the sterling will rise in the future, they will demand more now to be able to make a profit. This increase in demand will cause the value to rise. Therefore movements in the exchange rate do not always reflect economic fundamentals, but are often driven by the sentiments of the financial markets.

11. Balance of Payments

A large deficit on the current account means that the value of imports is greater than the value of exports. If this is financed by a surplus on the financial/capital account then this is acceptable. But a country who struggles to attract enough capital inflows will see depreciation in the currency. The exchange rate of the currency in which a portfolio holds the bulk of its investments determines that portfolio's real return. A declining exchange rate obviously decreases the purchasing power of income and capital gains derived from any returns.

Moreover, the exchange rate influences other income factors such as interest rates, inflation and even capital gains from domestic securities. While exchange rates are determined by numerous complex factors that often leave even the most experienced economists flummoxed, investors should still have some understanding of how currency values and exchange rates play an important role in the rate of return on their investments.